WEDNESDAY NOTES

Lucy Tobias is an author and blogger who looks at life and finds humor, beauty, and reasons for hope. As the pandemic produced panic, Tobias picked up a shovel and began digging a pond to stay sane. Did it work? The jury is still out.

Tobias also began Wednesday Notes, a weekly blog sharing the profoundness of everyday life. Spring, summer, fall and winter – the seasons for 2020 and 2021 are brought together in this book.

A mindful and timely read for the jaded of heart who might have forgotten, in our current chaos, how to believe in miracles – starting right in your own back garden.

READERS REACTIONS

"I absolutely love your Wednesday Notes while sitting at your dining room table . . .they are full of fun, new awareness and oh ....so....refreshing!!! –Yvonne Brown

"God bless you!! Your Wednesday Notes full of meaningful messages is just what I needed." –Anna Davis

"Hope you save these Wednesday Notes for a published book later on. They are great! –Jim Hunder

"I so enjoy your Wednesday musings on nature and art and philosophy." –Kate Singer

"I do so love your Wednesday Notes. Thank you for expanding my mind and world!" –Missy Myers

"Your Wednesday Notes brought a smile to my inside which shows on my face!!!" –John Faitel

"I cannot tell you of the pleasure I get from watching your garden evolve. The path is gorgeous, and your ponds are beautiful. The stories you tell about the battle between providing little lunches for the fauna and the purchasing of nets and hiding places for your little wards has comedy and tragedy in the same commentary. It is all worthy of great story telling." –Mike Kennedy

# Wednesday Notes

## Lucy Tobias

Sea Aster PRESS

To my mother, Lucy Maude Ord Beebe, who seeded the future by flinging poppy seeds into the wind as we traveled.

# Spring 2020

And so, it begins. The first wheelbarrow full of dirt – the start of an inground pond in my back garden.

Good thing the construction schedule is not etched in stone. There has been a setback. I noticed a Gulf fritillary caterpillar hanging on the underside of the wheelbarrow lip.

The caterpillar was on a mission to become a pupa (a chrysalis). And that change from caterpillar to pupa happens fast. The next day the top half looked like a dead leaf. The bottom half was still a caterpillar.

My goodness! I always thought butterflies went through metamorphosis in one pass – a caterpillar one day then oh, sometime later, a butterfly.

Not! The life change takes two stages. First the caterpillar turns into a pupa, looking like a dead leaf or whatever chrysalis shape works with that species of butterfly. Metamorphosis number one!

Then time passes. The dead leaf becomes transparent. Out comes a beautiful butterfly. And if you have ever witnessed this event, it is breath taking. Metamorphosis number two!

I still use the wheelbarrow, being careful not to disturb the pupa. It hangs down under the wheelbarrow lip. The adventure continues.

Meanwhile every American man, woman and child is stuck at home due to pandemic restrictions. Most are in their kitchens cooking. Works for me.

Last Sunday's New York Times had a recipe submitted by Florence Fabricant for a dish called Dutch Baby.

Who could resist this name? You will need a Dutch oven or any oven proof baking dish. 40 minutes total time. Serves three to four (or one person for two days breakfast)

Ingredients

3 eggs

½ cup flour (I used gluten free)

½ cup milk (I went with oat milk)

1 Tablespoon sugar

Pinch of nutmeg if you have it

4 Tablespoons unsalted butter (I used grass fed)

Syrup, preserves, confectioner's sugar or cinnamon sugar for toppings.

Directions

Heat oven to 425 degrees. Combine eggs, flour, milk, sugar and nutmeg in a blender jar and blend until smooth. Batter may also be mixed by hand.

Place butter in heavy 10-inch skillet or baking dish and place in oven. As soon as the butter has melted (watch so it does not burn) add batter to pan. Return pan to oven and bake 20 minutes until pancake is puffed up and golden. Lower oven temperature to 300 degrees and bake five minutes longer. Cut in wedges. Serve with topping of your choice.

In "normal" times I would have whined about using sugar. But these are difficult times. Bring on the maple syrup and powdered sugar, preferably organic. Please don't ask me why it is called a Dutch Baby. I haven't a clue. Do you?

Surely you have an extra carton or two of eggs in the refrigerator – right? You and I both know egg salad gets boring quickly.

Let's do something fun. I cooked three eggs in the Instant Pot on pressure cook setting for six minutes. The eggs sat on a trivet, and I added one cup of water. Outcome: perfect hardboiled eggs.

Then when the eggs cooled, I scrounged around for paint, easy to do when you are an artist. I came up with some acrylics and a white marking pen.

Sharpies would work too. Or crayons. Or watercolors. Obviously having an Easter egg dye kit is not on my shopping list in these days of essentials only (no kits on store shelves). Make do with what you have on hand.

Painting the eggs this morning brought back some wonderful memories of past Easter egg painting parties.

Call this project Double Duty Eggs – serving as food for lunch or dinner and fun in the meantime. One egg will end up tonight grated on top of salad. Others may top steamed vegetables tomorrow. And yours?

Digging the pond continues one wheelbarrow full at a time. The dirt is going along the fence line. So, if the deep end is supposed to be three feet deep, will I need a ladder to get down there and dig? Just wondering.

I fantasize that I have a gig for you, complete with social distancing. You sit under the umbrella and sip sun tea, watching me dig this pond hole some ten feet away from you – then we trade places, and you dig! Smile.

Meanwhile the pupa is still attached to the side of the wheelbarrow. Every day I check it out. Perhaps with a bit of serendipity I'll be there when the Gulf fritillary butterfly emerges. That would be awesome.

Right next to where the pond is being dug sits the veranda with a three-circuit contemporary labyrinth painted on it – adapted from a design by a Ringling School of Art student.

And recently a flamingo arrived. No, this bird is not an escapee from Jungle Gardens. It is a garden figure made of metal. Always wanted one.

Be willing to try new things.

Be the person who says WOW more than once today.

God bless the Queen of England, so dignified and calm. Hands folded in her lap; she sits up straight – the perfect picture of a woman from another age where posture mattered.

Wearing a green dress along with her signature three strands of pearls and a brooch that belonged to her grandmother, Queen Elizabeth delivers a four-minute speech. Her words radiate more hope for the future than any lengthy partisan pandemic briefings emanating daily from across the pond in America.

She said in part:

"We will succeed. Better days will return. We will be with our friends again. We will be with our families again. We will meet again."

Amen. As for the view from my window - a Buddha statue watches serenely as pond digging gets deeper. Contours are beginning to show.

Remember the pupa attached to the underside of the wheelbarrow lip? One morning I looked, and the pupa seemed smaller. Humm. Thought it was supposed to get bigger closer to transformation. In the afternoon I looked again. The pupa is gone. I could not find it in the grass.

Like life sometimes, the ending of this butterfly's life cycle is unknown. The same day the pupa disappeared I captured this photo of water drops on a lotus leaf.

Bending over to get a better look I saw movement on a rubber leaf that had fallen into the pond. Turns out to be tiny baby tadpoles! The frogs have been busy!

Changes occurring in my back garden. Changes transpiring with me. Every day I try to draw how I feel. Every day is different.

My lifesaving mask arrived. Thank you to Carman for making these. I've entered an alternative universe, ready or not. Here is today's drawing:

Simple things make a difference. Happy Earth Day. Mother Earth thanks you in advance for following the mantra – Recycle, Reuse, Renew.

One example: paper egg cartons torn to pieces and put in the bottom of a gardening pot – helps cut down on pot weight when having all soil, also provides aeration.

Want to record your Earth Day and everyday thoughts and drawings? One idea – a box journal designed by artist Carla Sonheim and demonstrated during (virtual) Sketchbookrevival2020. Start with a blank journal page. Draw a box around the four sides. Divide the box into sections.

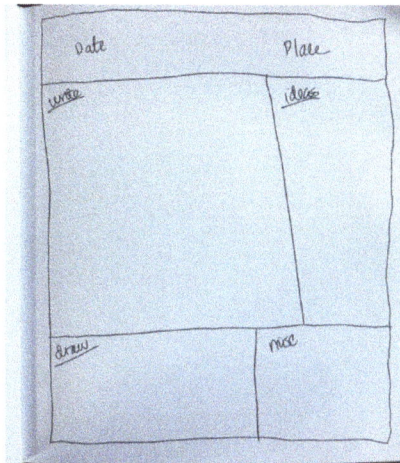

At the top write today's date on the left and where you are on the right. Label the sections. I'm sure your lines will be straighter than mine.

Write: put down your thoughts. I like to do this in the morning with first cup of coffee.

Ideas: thoughts lead to ideas and spinoffs. Also, a place to put lists, like ten things you love about your grandchildren or five things you like about yourself.

Draw: How do you feel today? Use simple lines. Maybe add the color of the day, the word of the day.

Misc.: this could be a wish list. Be inventive!

Meanwhile the pond keeps getting deeper – 15 inches deep now. Thought I'd go to 36 inches deep, but the work is hard. I'll be happy to make it to 30 inches.

Three people digging – me, myself, and I. We take turns.

Yesterday a Downy Woodpecker flew into my back garden. Yeah! Welcome, woodpecker.

Speaking of birds, can anyone explain to me why a Red-Bellied Woodpecker is called Red-Bellied when the only red to be found is on its head? One of life's mysteries.

Food. As lockdown continues food bills are rising, at least mine have. All about comfort food these days.

Pastor Wes Bixby of First Congregational United Church of Christ Sarasota even gave a sermon on Comfort Foods.

Did you know in a national poll pizza won first place as the best comfort food?

Who am I to argue with winners – so I made a pizza using cauliflower crust topped with organic steamed kale, grated organic mozzarella cheese and sauteed organic mushrooms. Did I mention the word organic enough times? Partnered the pizza with a glass of, you guessed it, organic wine.

Every project, making pizza, writing a book, or digging a pond, has a beginning, middle and end.

Beginnings are a rush, like falling in love, everything new and exciting, all things possible,

The middle of any project is just plain hard work. The beginning is in the rear view mirror. The popping of the champagne bottle at the end is nowhere in sight. Keeping motivated in the middle is difficult.

The middle. That is exactly where I am with digging the pond. Down to 18 inches at the deep end and so many more inches to go.

As a perk I took a break and bought a pail of rocks, picking out each one carefully. My goodness, rocks are heavy. The five-gallon pail when full weighed 33 pounds.

Why rocks? When the pond is dug, a liner goes in and extends over the sides. The sides are weighed down with rocks to keep the liner in place. Meanwhile, dig in.

Last Saturday there was a virtual worldwide finger labyrinth walk that included the idea of using our voice as we use our fingers to walk a labyrinth design.

Use words or chants. Find your own voice. Kay Barrett in England wrote an easy chant to sign as you walk the finger labyrinth. This is both a chant and a prayer:

All shall be well.

Do not be afraid.

Know you are loved.

May I have a drum roll please . . . digging an outdoor pond is done! Not as deep as I first envisioned but deep enough, 17 inches at the deep end, leveled on the bottom, sides sloped and ready for a pre-liner. Estimated capacity: 315 gallons.

I totally lost count of how many wheelbarrows full of dirt were removed. At times I feared my epitaph would read:

SHE NEVER STOPPED DIGGING

The next step is a pre-liner laid down to prevent roots and sharp things from tearing the liner. Many thanks to Greg C. for donating old throw rugs and drop cloths. I found a few old towels and a big beach towel to complete the task.

Coming soon: a pond filled with water. Then let it cure for a week. Add plants. Add fish. Begin the pond ecosystem. Why let it sit for a week? Water out of a hose contains chlorine. Chlorine kills fish. Letting a pond cure allows the chlorine to evaporate. Takes about three days but the recommended time for a total cure is seven days.

Meanwhile, inside, sitting on the living room couch, coffee in hand, I looked out the front windows and saw my first hummingbird.

No big deal, right? These bright green fast flyers are everywhere. Wrong.

In the eight years I've lived here in Sarasota I've never seen a hummingbird in my yard even though I've planted things to attract them like fire spike and firebush.

Both bushes have long tubular flowers. Hummingbirds like to stick their beaks in tubular flowers. I confess I've even put out a sugar water container for them, complete with red flower openings.

Ah, but the hardcore hummingbird purists say only plant flowers hummingbirds like, don't feed them sugar. But sometimes I subscribe to the school of . . . whatever works.

My first hummingbird here worked the red flowers on the jatropha tree planted just outside the living room.

Jatrophas are huge attractors for birds, bees, butterflies, and now a hummingbird. The trees are always full of pollinators. Wish I could take credit for planting these trees but no.

Credit goes to the contractors eight years ago who remodeled this small house built in 1952. They landscaped the front with two jatrophas and Mexican pentas. Thank you!

If you are looking to replace a tree, or plant a tree in a new place, think jatropha – it can be a bush or tree, depends on pruning. Has color year round and brings on the pollinators, all good.

My hummingbird (already I'm proprietary) came again the following morning, this time in my back garden as I sat with iced tea and listened to the pond fountains gurgle their water music.

My hummingbird (he? she?) worked the red tropical sage plant then moved on to the shrimp plant and finally flew across the garden to favor the firebush.

I've often wondered about hummingbirds – are they not around much or are we just not out and about at the right times?

Living in Ocala, I never saw them. But then I worked full time as a newspaper reporter.

Rising early one morning, just after dawn, I looked out the kitchen window and lo, two hummingbirds at the hummingbird feeder! Then they flew to the coral honeysuckle sprouting flowers over an arbor.

Bingo. It is all about being in the right place at the right time – looking out a window or being outside. Personally, I like the being outside option better.

Yet the pandemic has promoted (or did we just succumb?) to more personal computer time, checking social media, being at Zoom meetings, attending webinars.

Without a doubt the best webinar I've seen recently is Douglas Tallamy's talk, "A Guide to Restoring the Little Things that Run the World." Available on You Tube.

That video inspired a chapter called "Investing in Insects" in my book *The Zen of Florida Gardening*. Yes, insects are the little things that run the world. You can transform the world right now – where you live or at a nearby park. Plant mostly natives. This brings on the insects and they attract the birds. Change the world, one garden at a time.

Be well. Breathe deeply. Be kind to one another.

Months ago, in a leap of faith this day would come, I bought a 10 foot by 13 foot pond liner. Opening it up carefully, laid the liner over the pond. Then turn on the hose. And so, filling the pond begins.

What a difference it makes to add water! The pond, just a dream all these months, becomes real. It holds water!

Did you know water is heavy? One gallon of water weighs 8.3 pounds. This pond holds some 315 gallons of water. Do the math.

As the water rises, the liner begins to sink down in the hole. My job – stay vigilant, walk around the pond, straighten out wrinkles making sure there is plenty of liner going up and over the pond sides.

Within an hour, the pond was full.

As day ended and twilight took its turn a lovely refection of the nearby pine tree caressed the still water surface. Ah, a reflection pond! It is like a liquid mirror sending back images that change throughout the day.

If you'd like to see formal reflection ponds check out the elegant one at Alfred B. Maclay Gardens State Park in Tallahassee and the reflection pond in the Moonlight Garden at the Edison & Ford Winter Estates in Fort Myers.

Reflecting ponds were popular in ancient Persian gardens. The largest reflecting pond in the world is Miroir d'eau at Place de la Bourse in Bordeaux, France.

But alas, my small reflection pond will never make any travel list. It is temporary.

Still to come to the pond are plants, pump, fountain, and fish, all of which disturb reflections.

And don't forget the rocks. Lots of rocks around the edges. Then plants to fill the spaces between rocks. Do you have any plants that would be happy near a pond that gets full morning sun, say four hours a day?

Pass-alongs are perfect. Thank you in advance.

My cell phone vibrated (I keep the ringer off). A librarian calling from Selby library saying they were resuming pickup of books that were reserved. Would I like to make an appointment to get my two reserved books?

I was shaking with excitement. It has been so long since I saw an actual library book, I've quite forgotten what they look like.

Yes! Sign me up!

The drill: Drive to Selby. Stay outside in the car. Call to say you have arrived for your appointment. A librarian wearing mask and gloves comes out with a bag bearing my name. Places bag on table. Goes back inside,

I exit my car, wearing my mask, run to the table and grab the bag. At home I wipe the covers with paper towels sprayed with vinegar. And there you have the new pandemic look in library withdrawals.

My reads: *If You Were Here*, a mystery by Alafair Burke and *Essays 1969-1990* by Wendell Barry. Good reads.

Even with the pandemic somehow my datebook is filling up with Zoom meetings. There is a dress code developing. Put on earrings. Maybe even lipstick. And eyeliner.

Well, let's not get too carried away.

A jazzy top works, they are only seeing you from mid view up.

Tops these days are selling like hotcakes at a Saturday morning Kiwanis breakfast. Bottoms not so much.

In one Zoom meeting some said that perception is reality. Indeed, it is. I look good in earrings. That is my reality.

It has been a long time since Philosophy 101 in college. Still, it may be safe to say our perspective determines our reality. Here are three perspectives I like a lot:

All will be well. We are not alone. You are loved.

While sitting at my dining room table, passed down to me from my mother's family, I look out over my back garden. This is my go to destination for connecting with nature.

Today Gulf fritillaries do figure eights looking for passion vine (yes, I have some). A zebra longwing looks for passion vine too – also its host plant for laying eggs. Plus, a sulfur butterfly knows right where the cassia plants are located.

Swallowtails have once again discovered the exuberant pipevine taking over the back fence.

To identify the kind of swallowtail I opened my favorite Florida butterfly book, *Florida Butterfly Gardening* by Marc. C. Minno and Maria Minno. I discover this is a last stage caterpillar of a Polydamas butterfly.

A friend once confessed she liked butterflies but not caterpillars. Here is the good news/bad news – you can't have butterflies without caterpillars – all part of the life cycle.

And you can have the whole life cycle if you never, ever again use pesticides in your garden, plus plant host and nectar plants. Pesticides kill pollinators. This is bad.

A few years ago, Susan Lerner arrived for an interview to be director of horticulture at the Preservation Foundation of Palm Beach. She walked through their half-acre Pan's Garden to reach the Foundation's headquarters in an old historic building.

It was an unnerving walk.

"There was nothing flying, and I thought, where is everybody?" recalled Lerner.

No butterflies. No pollinators. No birds.

Lerner got the job. Then she discovered there was a pest control contract. That explained the lack of "everybody." The first thing she did as director of horticulture was to cancel the pesticide contract.

The results of no pesticides are impressive. I visited Pan's Garden a year later. Pollinators everywhere. And I saw, for the first time in my life, the caterpillars of an Atala butterfly, very rare, also known as coontie hairstreak.

Every butterfly gardener wants to see a butterfly emerge from a chrysalis. A small miracle. My moment arrived recently. This monarch is untouched by life. It had just emerged and was drying its wings before flying away. Serendipity is the intersection between coincidence and preparedness. May you have serendipity in your garden.

Greg Chestnut serves as Minister of Music at First Congregational United Church of Christ, Sarasota, Florida. He is also known as The Rock Man.

When traveling, Greg collects rocks. Every rock has a story. He builds cairns and labyrinth paths with these rocks.

I confess, what I know about rocks could fill a thimble. Rocks are old. They are heavy.

The Rock Man offered to help construct a rock waterfall at the new pond dug in my back garden. I quickly accepted.

Off we go to an amazing place called Total Landscape Supply with piles of rocks neatly separated by point of origin and colors. We pick them up gently, turning to see all sides embedded with striations of color – lovely pinks, oranges, ochres and burnt siennas.

Rocks come with cool names like Tennessee Sandstone, Sherry Tumbled and Euro Boulders, indicating the origin of these slices of the earth's crusts, small geological masterpieces.

We loaded up our carefully chosen rocks onto a rolling cart. Back home, rocks unloaded, I wisely step aside to sit, be quiet and drink homemade sun tea while The Rock Man works his magic, composing right on the spot.

Greg is a fan of Michael Grab. Watch one of Grab's videos where he defies gravity making huge cairns with no glue while standing knee deep in frigid northwest rivers. Grab looks for imperfections in rocks. How does he know an imperfection when he sees one?

Then, more mystery, Grab says what he does to build cairns is match one imperfection to another imperfection.

To me, a pile of rocks looks like random puzzle pieces that could never fit together. To Greg they are building blocks. Starting with a flat base The Rock Man builds upwards, placing a rock, then taking it away, trying angles, views – all with a goal to be structurally sound an appealing on all sides.

It did not take long. A rock sculpture took shape behind the birdbath placed at the end of the pond. From a long plastic tube that I'd installed earlier, water was pumped from the pond, trickled down the rocks, into the slightly tilted birdbath, then down into the pond.

As a finishing touch The Rock Man made a small five-stone cairn. Odd numbers like five and seven are supposed to be just right for cairns.

I learned a bit about rocks and a lot about how awesome it is watch creativity at work, one stone at a time. Thank you to The Rock Man.

Back inside sitting on the couch I reach for the Sunday New York Times. Haven't had a hard copy real paper in years – it seems we've already seen all the headlines on TV.

Now, in lockdown, I subscribe to the Sunday NYT. It takes me all week to read it all. I save the good stuff like the book review and magazine for last.

My friend Judy reads the book review and magazine first. Considering how depressing the news is, I'm thinking she has her priorities straight.

But that plan was impossible two weeks ago when the NYT gave the whole first page, and inside pages, to dead people. No photos. One thousand people out of the 100,000 people who died in the US so far from COVID-19.

Reporters researched every name and brought them alive in just a few words – name, age, place, and something about them: a musician, a doctor, maker of quilts, a lifelong volunteer, a CEO – so much love, compassion, community connections and life knowledge lost to this invisible enemy.

This is what newspapers do best – tell the rest of the story. Reporters researched newspapers around the country lifting death notices and obits of people who died from the virus. The result is tough reading but stunning journalism.

In the interests of full disclosure, I was a reporter for the New York Times regional group for 25 years, then retired. The NYT has since sold all its group papers.

Getting a paper again has broadened my stay at home horizons. I've tackled the easy crossword puzzles, made my own oat milk, cooked wonderful mac and cheese, inhaled stories of neighborhoods coping with lockdown, read opinions I did not like, and considered the plight of world class athletes trying to train for the Olympics.

Often words fail me when I read news about America tearing itself apart. When words fail, it is time for action.

Buckle up. I have an action – a mission – for you. Build a five or seven stone cairn.

A cairn on pathways is used as a marker. A cairn can be a memorial, a direction post, a waymark, a milestone.

Choose your stones carefully. Breathe deeply. Find the imperfection. Put one stone on top of another. If the cairn falls apart, rebuild.

Be reminded that everything is connected – you, the stones, the earth, yesterday, today, and tomorrow. Breathe deeply. Begin again.

I drive by Farm and Garden, a local garden shop in Sarasota, and see the parking lot is full.

Must be due to Plan B. When Plan A, the normal life we once knew, is gone, then go to Plan B – dig into the earth, get outside.

My friend Ceil in Tallahassee did just that. She has a large rectangular back yard, with corners, those 90-degree fence angles.

Very feng shui of Ceil to break up the 90-degree angles with a quarter-circle and plantings at each corner.

The term feng shui comes from China. It is an ancient tradition saying our lives are intertwined with the workings of nature (read: everything is connected).

The force that binds lives and nature together is ch'i or energy. Think of ch'i like water flowing down a stream. There are rocks in the stream. Over time, the flowing water works on the rocks, rounding off sharp corners, and the round corners make for good water flow – or energy flow.

So too in the garden. Rounding is good. Sharp 90-degree angles (called killing angles) are not.

Another example – this one from the Villages near Ocala at a home that has planted native plants. A screened veranda at the back of the home has two rounded planters, one outside each end of the veranda. Each planter has a huge fire bush, very attractive for pollinators. This is a lovely way to soften the 90-degree angles of the veranda.

Speaking of rounded – all three of my bird baths are rounded. While sitting at the dining room table I have a good sight line outside of St. Francis sitting next to one of the bird baths.

My casual bird viewing got a whole lot more interesting with the acquisition of a small pair of binoculars (12x26). When a bird lands on the bird bath, I pick up the binoculars, already calibrated for that distance. Suddenly the view is up close and personal.

A blue jay got seriously enthusiastic about bathing, throwing water in all directions. I could almost feel the water drops on the binoculars even though I'm inside and some sixteen feet away.

I envy that blue jay. How I wish I could get wet – go back to Warm Mineral Springs in North Port and soak a while.

But WMS is closed due to COVID-19. I don't know when going there will ever be possible again.

It occurs to me that the blue jay bathing in the bird bath has more freedom than I do right now.

If you have a bird bath, or are close to getting one, consider placing a stone near the edge or in the middle.

Perhaps get a rock with words etched. I like the one that reads: "begin again."

A stone makes it easier for butterflies to drink water. Butterflies can't afford to get their feet wet, but will land on a rock, unroll their proboscis and drink. Taking butterfly drinking to the next level – make a piddling pond – any container with wet sand and rocks on top. Butterflies need the minerals in the sand and the water.

You know you need a new project.

# Summer 2020

A slow morning walk around my back garden, coffee mug in hand, reveals nature unfolding one leaf at a time. I look closely at a new lotus leaf curled up in the small pond.

As the morning progresses this leaf opens to the warmth of morning sun.

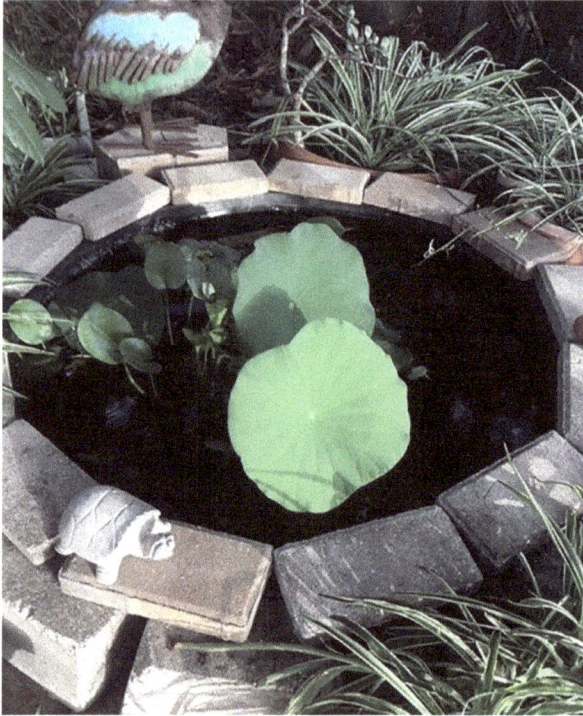

Ponds speak to me. I seek them out. Yesterday I traveled across the state to McKee Botanical Garden in Vero Beach. Never been. McKee was on my "to do" research for my book The Zen of Florida Gardening.

McKee is famous for their water lilies. Numerous ponds grace the sides of sidewalks here. Water lilies burst into bloom during the month of June.

Usually there is a water festival but not this year due to COVID-19. But you can visit and see the water lilies.

Decades ago, this garden was much bigger. Development ate away most of the garden acreage. Over time the gardens declined and closed. But a concerted effort in the 1990s saved this remnant now named McKee Botanical Garden.

Volunteers cleaning out thick debris in a clogged pond found a stone bridge. Seriously! Since then, weddings, graduations, countless selfies, even a few engagements all have happened on the stone bridge.

Even as we carry on in these difficult times, doing book research, cooking meals, digging ponds, there are some things we just don't need to know.

This week I found out that snakes can fly. Say it isn't so! There is a You Tube video as proof. Turns out flying snakes can be fascinating to some. At the start of the video a researcher says he spent ten years studying how snakes fly. Personally, I can think of better things to do with a decade of my life, but who am I to judge another's life choices?

The researcher posed this question – do snakes undulate while flying because they are snakes, and they undulate, or does this make a difference to flying? Inquiring minds want to know.

Setting up an experiment in a warehouse – a fake tree branch and a fake tree nearby for the snake to jump to.

The snake body was painted with high tech coating that can be captured on camera and turned into motion on a computer.

The experiment begins. People approach the fake tree branch with a snake. Naturally the snake wants to leave, go elsewhere. It launches off into space, undulating, and lands in the tree.

Watching the video afterwards the snake's glide (flying) is helped by undulating, a motion that maintains stability. Without undulating, the snake would just fall out of the tree branch and land on the ground. Splat. Who knew?

Knowledge is power but that does not mean I want to add looking up at snakes in trees as something I want to add to my "to do" list. These times are difficult enough already without adding snakes.

After three months of lockdown, time to take our pulse. My heart rate goes up when I'm out in public. Even though I wear a mask I worry someone will cough near me or laugh at me for wearing a mask.

I am afraid. The object of my fear is something I cannot see or define, namely the virus. Fear lives, not in my head, but in my gut. It drains energy.

And living with this fear, I begin for the first time to understand my brothers and sisters of color – and how they feel every time they step outside their homes to live their lives.

Fear they will be arrested because of their color. Fear they will not come home.

Fear is corrosive, consuming and debilitating. I had no idea. Now I have an inking.

"The earth laughs in flowers." Ralph Waldo Emerson's words. Laughter is good. So, flowers are today's topic.

I found nasturtiums growing outside the historic mission in Carmel, California. These flowers do wonderfully well year round in California. Nasturtiums grow in Florida but can die back in the sultry summer.

Nasturtiums are edible. Yes! Both flowers and leaves. The flowers taste like lemon pepper. Awesome on top of steamed vegetables and salads.

Once in Ocala when my daughter-in -law visited, I gave her a bowl to go out and pick nasturtium flowers for various dishes. This was a first for her. Turned out to be a hit. Ah, score one for the mother-in-law.

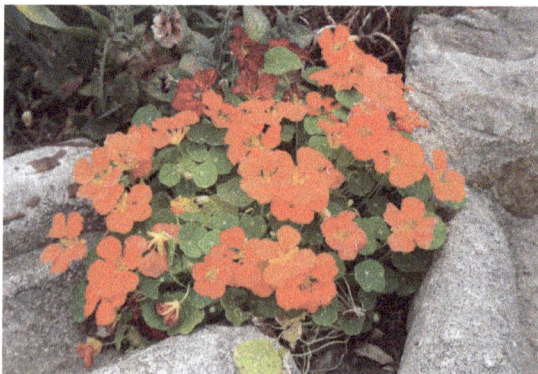

One day I saw a Great Southern White butterfly in my Sarasota back garden. Naturally, I wanted to know what kind of host plants they like. Turns out that nasturtiums will do. I promptly bought lots. Never did see caterpillars on the nasturtiums. But I am ready for Great Southern Whites.

While visiting the Seville area in downtown Pensacola I had lunch at a restored antebellum home.

There was a window box along the railing, right next to my outside table. Purple petunias were looking at me. I could almost hear them whisper: "What's for lunch?"

At the Fruit and Spice Park in Homestead, Florida I always gravitate to the ponds. No surprise there. Why else would I spend two months digging a pond?

It was here, in the water lily area, years ago, that I became inspired to include water lilies in my back garden.

The new pond that I dug and filled with water has a water lily. It must be happy. Every day or two flower stalks raise their heads to the sun and unfurl into full bloom. In the afternoons, almost like being on a timer, they furl back up again. Repeat the next morning.

Soothing to see these water lilies especially when combined with the sound of falling water from the fountain.

There is something magical about sunflowers. But I never brought any home, or any cut flowers, as my cats will try to eat them. Flowers grown in nurseries are sprayed with toxics. Naturally, the cats threw up.

Happily, the downtown Sarasota Farmers market has a vendor with organic sunflowers. I can bring them home and brighten up the kitchen without fear of harming the felines.

Roses are not my thing. But many gardeners embrace them. Like Mary Jane Leu, wife of Harry P. Leu – yes, that Leu of Leu Gardens in Orlando, Florida.

Mary Jane planted the first roses on their 50-acre property. After the property was donated to the city in 1961 other rose enthusiasts stepped up and started digging. There are over 215 varieties in Mary Jane's Rose Garden all suited to Central Florida.

Mable Ringing also had a thing for roses. Before any development took place on what is now the 66-acre John and Mable Ringling Museum of Art site in Sarasota, Florida, Mable had the rose garden finished in 1913, twelve years before their house (mansion) was built. The entire site was donated to the state in 1936.

The rose garden is a wagon wheel design patterned after a traditional Italian garden plan. Her original plants are all gone. Mable's garden was restored in 1991, again in 2004 and most recently in 2020. It is the only mini rose test garden in Florida.

On Mondays the Museum of Art and Bayfront Gardens are free admission. This is a good time to walk the grounds, check out Mable's Rose Garden and the heirloom roses.

Ah, I see eyebrows going up. Lucy is suggesting going somewhere in these COVID-19 times. Only do what is comfortable for you. But I've noticed, while doing research for my Zen Garden book, that botanical gardens are not well attended. No crowds.

Beaches and restaurants are getting the traffic. Outdoor places with different flowers that bloom every month of the year are being ignored. Just saying . . .

Meanwhile raccoons made another nighttime visit. Frogs laid more eggs in the big pond. The tadpoles in the little pond have turned into frogs, my passion vine is depleted. Send more passion vine (just kidding, maybe not).

Breathe deeply. Inhale fresh air. Exhale sadness.

Repeat as needed.

Simple things can make me smile. Like my spiralizer –
put in a zucchini or yellow squash, twist, and out comes
spaghetti spirals! Instant pasta without the grains. Works for me.

And sun tea. Two family size tea bags added to a one or
two quart glass container. Let brew outside in the morning sun.
Add mint if you have some in your garden. When nicely brewed
to a lovely shade of red brown, pour in a glass, add ice cubes
and a squeeze of lemon. Smile.

I'm sure you have simple things that make you smile and
enrich your day.

Important to know life can be good on this hot, humid
July summer day with COVID-19 cases spiking again in Florida,
the president finally wearing a mask – what took trump so long?
Lower case for president and trump is intentional.

And for sheer stupidity the governor of the state of
Florida said that going to school is like going to Walmart, so
open the schools.

Sometimes, way too often actually, it is downright
embarrassing to live in the sunshine state where politics is
completely divorced from reality.

But it is never embarrassing to step out into my back garden. Always something exciting happening like a cloudless giant Sulphur butterfly caterpillar seen this morning on the cassia plant.

And squinting closely at the small pond I see frogs' eggs shimmering on the surface – future tadpoles and frogs!

In the larger world, a great light has passed. John Lewis died from pancreatic cancer. John Lewis (1940-2020) was a civil rights leader, Congressman, author of *Walk with the Wind: A Memoir of the Movement* and a graphic novelist.

Here is a John Lewis quote, from a tweet:

"Do not get lost in a sea of despair," Lewis tweeted almost exactly a year before his death. "Do not become bitter or hostile. Be hopeful, be optimistic. Never, ever be afraid to make some noise and get in good trouble, necessary trouble. We will find a way to make a way out of no way."

Tell me that you too have done all these pandemic projects – cleaned out the cupboards, washed the floors, thinned out clothes in the closets, rearranged living room furniture yet again, bought too much stuff online, tackled the garage but retreated in defeat. The garage is that bastion of last resort where everything without a place elsewhere goes to rest for eternity.

Surely you need another project. How about your mailbox? That necessary but neglected necessity that is begging for an upgrade.

Mailboxes are hope incarnate. Today maybe the mailman or mailwoman will open the box and put in real mail – a letter from a friend, a card from family, something hand addressed with your name.

Alas, most days are doomed to disappointment. What arrives are political advertisements, letters from realtors wanting to buy your home, cheap rates on cremation, flyers with coupons to places you have no desire to visit, and way too many ads for hearing aids. Sigh.

And yes, hope springs eternal. Give your mailbox a makeover. I walked around my neighborhood looking at mailboxes and came home inspired.

If you live in a gated community where all mailboxes must be lined up exactly alike this makeover won't work for you but read on and enjoy the ride.

A basic mailbox comes in black or white. Functional but boring. Step it up by adding color, a mailbox magnetic design that drapes over the box – and can be changed with the seasons. You get the idea. Still the same box dressed up and ready to party.

Look at the ground around a mailbox. Think easy care, low water natives. But try not to plant bee friendly plants – your mail delivery person thanks you. They do not want to open the box and get stung by a bee.

Kicking up the mailbox makeover up one more notch – this mailbox seen in my neighborhood became a mosaic project. The result is stunning.

Ditching the traditional mailbox post can lead to dramatic results, like a flamingo or a manatee.

Take a walk around your neighborhood and look at mailboxes. And keep hoping for a personal letter.

And find a way to add these John Lewis words into your life. They continue to gather strength with each passing day. Here are some of his thoughts on life and love:

"You are a light. You are the light. Never let anyone – any person or any force – dampen, dim or dimmish your light. Study the path of others to make your way easier and more abundant. Lean towards the whispers of your own heart . . . Release the need to hate, to harbor division and the enticement of revenge. Release all bitterness. Hold only love . . ."

The view. Yes, it is a television show. It is also what you see out your window or standing outside. This is your real world!

Changing the view can be as easy as taking a day trip. And so, Bella, my rescue dog, and I went to Philippi Creek Park. For the first time we ventured on a forest path. Delightful. Different.

At the start is a tree with one limb growing straight out like it wants to cross the road and see the other side.

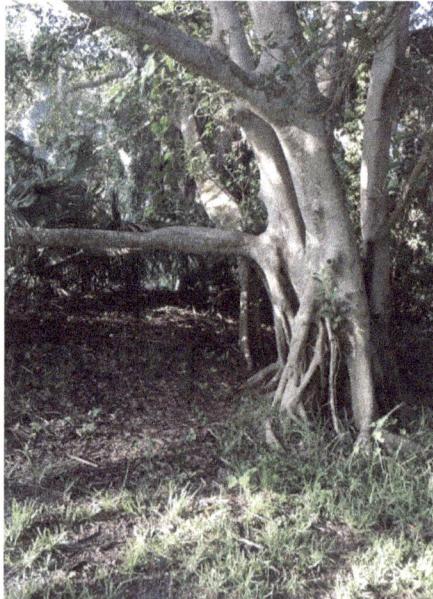

The view. For some, the perfect view takes place at the beach. Fortunately, there is a beach less than five miles away. When my horizons are feeling constrained by the pandemic or just everyday life, I head for the beach and look out over the Gulf of Mexico. Equilibrium restored. It helps to hear gently breaking waves.

Last week was redo your mailbox week. Gated communities require all mailboxes to be the same and readers were quick to respond.

Alleyne said: "I only wish we could improve on our mailbox. Not to be, Association rules . . .bah, humbug. Ahh, maybe I could leave something inside the mailbox, for the mailperson??? You always get me thinking!"

Thank you, Alleyne. What a great idea. You got me thinking. A mail person is indeed a first responder, out there every day, handing mail, saying safe, wearing gloves and mask. I need to find a way to say thank you to my mail person!

Jeanelle wrote that she had already upgraded her mailbox then went down the street and helped a neighbor redo hers. Ah, lets stir up the whole neighborhood.

Another way to stir up the neighborhood and make a difference – plant butterfly plants in unused spaces, like between a fence line and the curb. Butterflies need nectar and host plants.

A few blocks down from me, on city land near a curb, a local gardener got permission from the city to plant butterfly plants. They are doing well, and butterflies are frequent visitors.

Making a difference takes many forms. Like getting up in the morning and deciding to be joyful (instead of sad). Not only impacts your day but everyone you encounter, both live and virtual, will have some of that joy rub off on them.

My day starts, rain or shine, with feet on the floor by 5 a.m. The morning routine: Let the dog out into my fenced back yard. Turn on the coffee water. Feed two indoor cats. Let the dog back in. Feed the dog. Make coffee.

Note: I am the last in line to get any service in the morning. I have been well trained by my fur/fin family to put them first.

Finally, I make it to my comfortable chair and wrap both hands around a coffee mug. My drink is bulletproof style with grass fed butter added and brain octane oil added along with a dash of coconut milk to make it a bit white.

I take a deep sigh. This, ladies, and gentlemen, is my HOUR OF POWER. The quiet time may only last thirty minutes but that first cup of coffee is perhaps the best part of my day.

But I'm not done with daily duties. As the sun rises, I step outside in back garden, container of fish food in hand. Must feed the goldfish. They are already at the surface of the ponds, gulping air, acting like they've never been fed before. Goldfish are drama queens.

When my in the ground pond was finished and the water cured (no chlorine) I brought home six two-inch goldfish from a pet store. Now, two months later, they have more than doubled in size.

Did you know that goldfish, and koi, both members of the carp family, will grow to the size that fits their container? This new pond is 315 gallons, give or take, so we shall see.

Their growing up is iffy. Real life can be sunlight and water music but there may also be marauders – unannounced visits by great blue herons, great white egrets, raccoons, and other wildlife – all bent on destruction or dinner, whichever comes first. Goldfish are on the menu.

That is why I buy the cheap feeder fish (the kind some fish owners buy to feed their piranhas). I tell my fish they were spared. And I hope the wildlife won't show up and prove me wrong.

The fish feeding continues. I have two fish tanks inside the house, one with a betta and one with neon tetras. Fish are my motif, a theme that runs from live fish in tanks to a fish print by an artist friend hanging in pride of place on my living room wall.

Moving to Sarasota eight years ago I downsized considerably, shrinking to a 910-square foot house. I vowed to live by the mantra "LESS IS MORE" including less maintenance. And how is that working out?

Well, so far, I've installed three ponds outside, all need maintenance. I have one dog and two cats, all need maintenance.

Oh, and I didn't even mention the birdfeeder and birdbaths, all need maintenance.

By now you have figured out that extended family, fur, fins, feathers, and all, is my thing. You can blame it on my kids. They grew up and left home and well, I acquired a new family.

The maternal instinct runs deep.

Where do you go to meditate? A room with a view? The veranda? A deeply comfortable chair? Poolside? A labyrinth? The bathroom? The shoreline? A coffee shop?

My back garden is my go-to meditation spot. Morning coffee outside when the weather is cooler is like a mini-Sabbath and has rules.

No cell phone no electronics (like the radio my neighbor on the other side of the fence is currently playing). No newspapers or books. Just be. Remember once again that everything is connected – you, birds, bees, trees, flowers, all links in the ecosystem of life, all needing each other.

It never hurts to ramp up positive vibes for meditation. That is why I have three Buddha statues, one angel statue and one St. Francis statue in my garden. Lots of positive energy.

About the three Buddhas: One Buddha statue sits in the curve of a path. The curve was not wide enough for a paver and I found a Buddha statue that fits the space, perfect curve.

My smallest Buddha sits in a pot with a vinca plant. The largest Buddha anchors the 120-gallon preformed pond on my veranda. This one came from a garage sale. The tenants next door moved out, holding a garage sale before leaving. To my surprise they had four Buddhas lined up in a row. One came home with me.

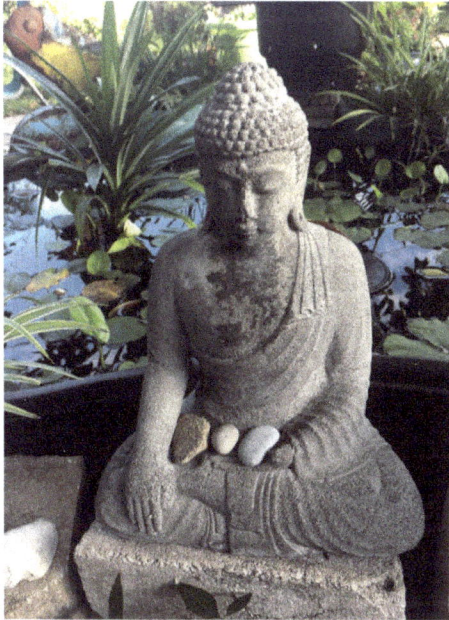

Most Buddhas have one hand that is open, flat outstretched. This is to signify a willingness, an openness, to whatever life must give – the open hand is ready to receive.

Do you have a Buddha in your life? Might consider getting one. We need all the good energy we can get.

Remember all those wheelbarrows of dirt dug up to make an in the ground pond? Well, that dirt became a berm running along a fence line.

And volunteer plants arrived. A lot of candlestick cassia, milkweed and who knows what else have taken seed and sprouted. Butterflies fluttering around that area have increased greatly.

I'm not around all the time. Yesterday I worked as a poll worker in the Primary Election. It was a sixteen-hour day. Really long. But satisfying. Voter turnout in the precinct I worked at was just over 600 people, much more than the 350 I had guessed would show up.

Voters are energized. Being involved, caring enough to vote, is a good thing. There is another election in November.

Just a heads up: if you request a vote by mail ballot, I honestly can't recommend putting it in the mail. These days USPS is toxic. Take your ballot to the Supervisor of Elections office or take to any drop-off point that takes ballots. These places will be on the Supervisor of Elections website for your county. Offer to make a ballot run and turn in all your family and friends' ballots.

Personal delivery of a vote by mail ballot means you have less exposure to large numbers of people in a polling place and you make sure your ballot is received.

YES, YOUR VOTE MATTERS. Believe it.

In the small pond a lotus is getting ready to bloom. Ah, anticipation – Merriam-Webster dictionary says this about anticipation:

The act of looking forward: visualization of a future event or state. That is me waiting for the lotus to bloom.

I suspect it is anticipation that is keeping us going these days – anticipating a flower blooming, a meeting outdoors with family or friends, a Zoom coffee hour after virtual church, a loaf of bread baking in the oven.

Meanwhile, where do you meditate? That was last week's question in Wednesday Notes.

Peggy replied: "Meditating . . .well, I get up at 5:20 a.m. go to morning mass, come home, eat, and then prepare supplies for a large painting." (Peggy is an awesome artist who is often commissioned to do large works for a church, a story in itself).

Patricia said: "You've seen where I meditate. My backyard. It is so peaceful looking out over the water. Except for last night when there was the worse lightning I've ever seen. I levitated out of my chair on one strike. Thought my house had been hit, it was so close and loud. Not too peaceful then."

Today your task is to go forth and look for purple. Look up. Look down. Look all around. Take notes. Let me know what you find. And don't forget to breathe.

Inhale the good.

Exhale the bad.

Repeat as needed.

Anticipation, such a lovely feeling, now replaced by awe and amazement. The lotus in the small pond is in bloom! Elated!

Meanwhile along the back fence line, pipevine is thick with leaves, flowers, and munched areas. Pipevine is a host plant for swallowtail butterflies. I turned over a leaf and saw baby swallowtail caterpillars clustered together. Munch away. Grow. Become butterflies. And thank you for being in my back garden!

My garden reveals life's journey with beginnings, in-betweens, and endings – all unfolding with quiet delicacy. I am humbled and honored to bear witness to this journey every day.

Recently Jennifer Huber, president of the Florida Outdoor Writers Association challenged members to write a haiku, an unrhymed poem, on how they spent their summer. She reminded us that traditional Japanese haiku (started in the 17th century) has five syllables in the first line, seven syllables in the second line and five syllables in the third line. I accepted the challenge and here is my haiku:

Empty chairs at home

Goldfish flash in the moonlight

Summer sings goodbye.

A school of modern American haiku thinks that the 5/7/5 syllable thing that works in Japanese just does not cut it in English. So American haiku could be three short unrhymed lines any which way you wish.

Plus, there is the thought that all haiku, however written, should spiral from a present small moment outward and include nature and seasons. Not everyone agrees that nature should be in there but that is why there are so many variations to the haiku theme.

I encountered the nature version in a writer's conference at Daytona Beach. Signed up for a class in American haiku. We gathered at café tables near a beach.

The teacher was late. He arrived sporting tattoos, retro 60's hippy garb including gold earrings and a big messenger bag slung over one shoulder.

With that look, we were at a loss what to expect. Maybe that was the point. With little adieu, he directed us to take off shoes, walk on the beach – walk slowly, look closely, be silent. Pick up a small shell or whatever appealed. Bring back the treasure trove in fifteen minutes.

Then, after a short talk about how a three-line haiku spirals out from a moment to the larger picture that includes the season and can even expand to the universe and the stars – he gave us all blank paper. We started writing.

We wrote and wrote and wrote. Like a geyser shooting upward, pent up energy desperate to be free, we wrote lots of haikus.

Then we read our poems out loud. Personally, I was stunned we could tap into this level of creativity so quickly. But we did. The teacher stood there smiling. Mission accomplished.

Your turn. Haiku anyone?

Who knew goldfish were drama queens? Not me. But I'm finding out they all have an advanced degree in drama.

Every morning I step out onto my veranda, food can in hand. The goldfish are lined up at the surface of each pond, acting like they have never been fed and starvation is imminent.

Their act is very convincing. Company loves it. But I'm not fooled. Life is good for those with fins. The goldfish know it. They just won't admit it.

Perhaps the goldfish will write a watery haiku about food and the universe.

After last week's call for haiku, traditional or American, readers were quick to respond. Linda wrote: "What fun! Here are my two attempts. Remember it is fall in Michigan."

Fall gulls take the shore

Whitecaps thunder on the beach

Spray kisses my face


Squirrels busy digging

Acorns bombing on the railing

Fall is in the wings


Joanie and Phillip were about to embark on a RV trip to the Smoky Mountains. Wheels up at 5:55 a.m. She wrote:

Georgia let us in . . .

Rest areas are closed

Blue sky – no clouds

Kate in England said she was no good at sticking to the confines of a proper Japanese Haiku but was inspired to contemplate and describe nature. Here is her haiku:

School bus takes boys to a new unknown

Quiet descends on the house

Late summer breezes sigh through the sycamore.

Once, long ago, we filled our calendars with no thought that a pandemic would reduce our days to empty calendar pages.

And yet, with all that time comes a new appreciation of simple chores. Like snipping off the ends of green beans then cutting to length. Snip. Cut. Repeat. The pile of uncut beans gets smaller. The pile of cut beans gets bigger.

Repetitive work is somehow satisfying. Maybe that is why knitting is so popular.

Back to the beans – snip, cut, cook, and eat. Works for me. And besides I just like sitting on the bar stool at the kitchen prep table. Two cats and one dog are nearby. In case something edible falls off the table, the cleanup crew is on the job.

Mostly I do the beans, preferably organic, for Bella. Good for her digestive system. Not bad for mine either.

How wonderful it is to have a dog in my life again. Two months ago, I adopted a rescue, a mutt, mostly lab, found as a stray. Perhaps five to six years old, a female who has had babies (no more). She did not come with a file folder tucked under one paw detailing name, lineage, food preferences. So truly a new beginning for both of us.

A new life. A new name. Bella. She is beautiful, what can I say? I'd repeat her name and she'd look around, puzzled, but in less than a week – she knew her name.

Bella came housebroken (thank goodness), knows words like breakfast, cookie. Can sit on command and shake one paw. Who would give her up? She is sweet and gets along with the cats. Her tail wags a lot.

Bella loves to ride in the car but hates to get out of the car and go for a walk. I'm a walker so this is going to take a deep breath. The shelter manager thinks she (and another dog that might have been a daughter or sister) were taken for a ride in a car then dumped in a park.

That explains why she is afraid of traffic and loud noises.

Bella loves to cuddle, take naps, chill, pay with squeaky toys. A friends said Bella was looking for me long before I found her. Could well be true.

Simple really. Bella needs me. I need to be needed. So two paws up to Bella and all the dogs that enrich our lives with their unconditional love.

A few weeks back I asked readers to look for purple in their lives. Sandra responded:

"A purple velvet pillow filled with lavender, good for warming up to put on aching muscles. Dramatic purple clouds in a painted landscape of the Sangre de Cristo Mountains, purchased in Taos last year, recently framed, and awaiting placement on the wall. Purple peppers from our garden, suffering from the  heat, too soft to eat."

Lovely.

Look for colors in your life.

Ah, fall is in the air. I can feel the coolness on my skin. There is a slight lifting to the humidity. Air feels lighter, brighter, and invigorating.

Bella feels it too. She is frisky, prancing around. I know just how she feels. Sure, the calendar said Tuesday was the first day of fall. But it isn't fall until your DNA sings with gratitude – Alleluia! Hot summer days are done! A day like today with temperature in the 70s for early morning.

Goodbye summer. Hello fall, Florida style.

Baking bread and fall go well together. But then I've had a long standing love affair with baking bread. I wrote an introduction to bread for a newspaper employee cookbook and here it is:

"My parents did not bake bread. Neither did my grandparents, aunts, or uncles.

So here I am, born into a family without bread genes, yet inebriated with the smell of yeast, the slow deliberate process of kneading, the magic of bread rising in the pan.

I'm the woman who hand-carried a 20-year old batch of sourdough starter (a gift) from Seattle, Washington as we moved to Gainesville, Florida, cradling it in the front passenger seat of an International Travelall.

In Gainesville, my small children built block castles on the kitchen floor as bread rose on top of the stove. The smell of bread rising mingled with the laughter of children and I thought, it doesn't get any better than this.

That sourdough starter is long gone. Children are grown and gone, replaced by three cats and a dog sitting on the kitchen floor. But they do not build block castles or laugh as they play.

Bread still rises, gets punched down, rises again, part of an ancient ritual that ties me to desert wanderers and palace chefs.

We perform a rite that ends when family and friends sit down to break bread together.

And I think: it doesn't get any better than this."

Fast forward to now. I'm trying to make a sourdough starter. I can practically taste a good piece of toast with morning coffee. But I'm out of practice, it will take some trial and error. Like life, baking bread is a process.

Speaking of process, have you ever seen a resurrection fern? This amazing plant goes through a life and near death process on a regular basis.

The National Wildlife Federation says:

"The resurrection fern is a type of epiphytic fern, which means it grows on top of other plants or structures and reproduces by spores, not seeds. The spores are housed in structures called sori on the underside of fronds. Although resurrection ferns grow on top of other plants, they do not steal

nutrients or water from their host plant."

Among other places, resurrection ferns like to live on the upper side of oak tree branches. When rain is scarce the ferns shrivel up, look dead. In fact, one wonders why the fern doesn't just fall off the branch.

But it is waiting. Waiting for rain, preferably nice, steady, soaking rain. Then the resurrection begins., The fern comes back to life, green and vibrant. When the dry season begins, the fern shrivels up.

It is a process.

Sitting in my back garden next to a pond is a small mermaid statue. It is ceramic, a reproduction of the famous The Little Mermaid, a bronze statue by Edward Eriksen, showing a mermaid becoming human. And that idea was based on the title The Little Mermaid, a fairy tale by Hans Christian Andersen.

The Little Mermaid statue was unveiled in 1913. It is displayed on a rock by the waterside at the Langelinie promenade in Copenhagen, Denmark.

I've never seen the real statue, but it is cool to know I have a bit of hand me down history in my back garden. What history is in your garden?

And I can't resist one more pass at purple. When looking for purple in her life Pattie said: "I wondered where the purple is in my life . . .Oh, I'm wearing it."

Good one Pattie.

This morning's walk was a fall delight. Often wrong, the weather prediction turned out to be right – cold front.

A Florida style cold front namely temps in the low 70s. Long sleeve weather.

I can tell the seasons by my latte order. I went for a latte after my walk and the barista gave me a choice – iced or not?

Just to have a choice means summer is over, fall has arrived. Well, it may be brisk, but it is not that cold yet.

Iced it still is. Forward into fall.

Be outside.

Be kind to yourself.

Be well.

# Fall 2020

Have you read Michelle Obama's book *Becoming*? An outstanding book ripe with vivid descriptions of growing up, the support of family, friends, and teachers.

Later in life you can feel her pain coming off the pages. For example, when she describes the cruel treatment of her and her family by Hillary Clinton during the election race.

I walked outside into the back garden yesterday morning. Five water hyacinths were getting ready to bloom, not open yet, but close. The first word I thought of was "becoming" like Michelle Obama's book.

When they bloom, water hyacinths last a day or two, that is it. I am grateful to be here when they do. The back garden is evolving (becoming). I'm also evolving and yes, becoming. So are we all!

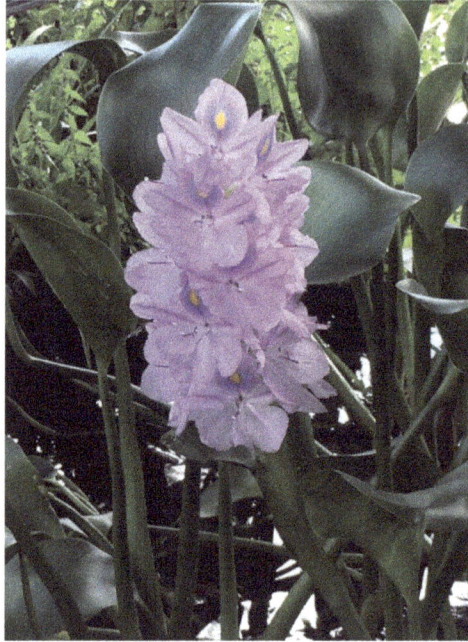

Certainly, life is different now than seven months ago. The rhythm and rhyme of daily life has changed.

On Wednesday evenings I sometimes sing in a Zoom choir rehearsal, much different than being in the church choir room.

Soon there will be a small Sunday service outside – bring your own chair, wear masks, social distance. No singing. No plans to open the church sanctuary to services anytime soon.

Happenings I once took for granted, like being a poll worker in the next election, no longer apply. For the first time in eight years, I've turned down the assignment of working an election, namely the November election.

I think highly of my co-workers and totally believe in the process of voting (despite obstacles).

My advice: Vote as if your life depended on it. For this election that may literally be true.

But the unknowns for a poll worker are daunting – being in a closed polling room all day with threats – COVID, unmasked coughing voters, the fall flu, the threat by trump (lower case intentional) to put troops at polling places, not to mention I'm getting a bit long in the tooth to be working 14-16 hour days. Time to resign and move on.

The Old Testament says: "To every thing there is a season." (Ecclesiastes 3:1). Working the polls – the season has passed.

Holiday gatherings cancelled. That season is gone unless we can figure out how to do it all safely outside.

But life abhors a vacuum and so when a thing is ended, its place is taken by new things, new seasons.

We are in a season where we can have stillness to our days, an appreciation of being here now, an inhaling of fresh fall air outside, gratitude to be able to hug a dog when hugging people is out of the question, a time to gather memory moments like seeing a water hyacinth in bloom.

When in doubt, take a deep breath.

Go forth into your days with gratitude for this season.

Eva the cat stares at shadows on the living room floor. The shadow of a lizard on the window moves. She reaches out and tries to grab the shadow.

Shadow play. Afternoon sun comes in the living room floor to ceiling windows, bright light on the floor showing shadows of tree branches, a passing lizard going across the window screen.

Go for the shadow! Watching Eva reminds me of childhood games at night. We'd turn a bright light onto a wall and play shadow puppets. Did you ever do that? A cheap thrill, homemade fun, before iPads and phone texting took over the world of children and adults.

Meanwhile flowers in my back garden are blooming – water hyacinths, Mexican sunflowers, and pagoda plants, all plants passed on as gifts from one person's garden to mine.

It surprised me to learn pagoda plants are members of the mint family. These outlandish blooms attract pollinators, especially butterflies.

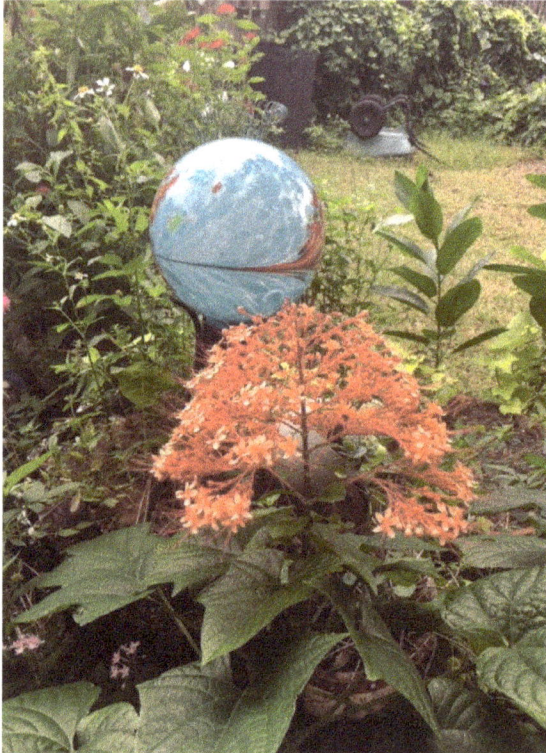

Moving from pagoda plants to patches and medals.

My son Chris figured out I like the medals that go with finishing a race or other sports event.

He is currently into rucking. Ruckers do insane things like climb stairs with a backpack weighing 40 pounds. No wonder their nickname is "wierdos."

Recently Chris took on a Ruck challenge of climbing 3,960 stairs. Why that number? Each of the Twin Towers was

110 stories tall. That is 1960 steps per tower. Walk the total number of stairs for both towers and get a patch.

Chris says they sent him two patches by mistake (like I'm buying that) and would I like to take the challenge and earn a patch?

I don't even have to ruck, just climb stairs. Well, to my credit, I did not say yes right away. Instead, I asked myself – where in Sarasota will I find stairs accessible to the public?

And I'm finding them. Two downtown parking garages with six flights each. Sure, there are elevators. There are also stairs that are open to outside views. It feels safe to walk them – stores and offices nearby.

I said yes. I'm counting backwards. So far, I am down from 3,960 stairs to 2,542 stairs in two weeks. At this rate by the time I finish I will be old and grey. Oh, wait . . .

As an aside, who knew it was all about Velcro these days? Chris sent me a cap with Velcro on the front. When I earn the patch, I'll Velcro it onto the cap.

In another lifetime, long ago and far away, my mom sewed my Girl Scout patches onto a green sash.

Put away the needle and thread. Velcro has taken over the world. The patch is calling to me. Time to climb more stairs.

Your turn.

Take on a challenge.

Treat yourself well.

Tune in next Wednesday.

Reconnecting with friends who have been out of sight for a while is an ongoing pandemic project for me.

So, it is a joy to reconnect with Herb Hiller, placemaker, writer and lecturer who lives in Deland, Florida. We met years ago at a Society of American Travel Writers conference. I clearly remember how Herb challenged me to think outside the usual travel writing box. I'm still trying to live up to his challenge.

The word placemaker is part of Herb's signature at the end of his email. A new word for me.

What is a placemaker? For that matter what makes a place a place? People? Natural surroundings? Signage? Tourism? Word of mouth? Zip code? Industry? Does a sign on the road saying Sarasota make it so?

Do travel writers like myself become placemakers when we write a story about a place? I asked Herb. His answer:

"The best travel writing is always about the integrity of places and, given my propensity, to act out my thought through advocacy beyond arguments."

In an article for Planeta.com Herb added:

"Place represents an orientation to wherever we find ourselves. This can be as close to home as a neighborhood we haven't come to know well – perhaps even our own with whose history and, except for its most routine patterns, with even its day to day life we are unfamiliar."

I get that. So do you, dear readers as you join me every Wednesday for a journey that orients us, like a compass, to where we find ourselves, I most often find myself in my back garden. Here I dig up soil, find surprises, sooth stress with water music, have adventures and escape from pandemic fatigue that dulls emotions, especially  happy ones.

By extension, walking around my neighborhood makes me realize I don't know it well even after eight years. Plus, the hood is evolving (becoming?).

New landscaping in front yards, a concrete driveway now done with pavers, houses painted, pools added. Easy to think this is all COVID 19 stay at home projects.

Still, by slowing down and walking around my neighborhood I find myself more oriented and orientation, a sense of knowing where you are, is a good thing in these chaotic times.

There is another level of place making – a collection of places that are sacred spaces. That would be labyrinths.

I spent twelve months walking labyrinths in Florida, research for my book *Circle the Center Labyrinths in Florida*.

And I've painted a three-circuit contemporary labyrinth on my veranda.

Labyrinths are ancient walkways, usually spirals that trace the journey of our lives. A labyrinth is not a maze. You cannot get lost. One path in, the same path journeys out.

To have a labyrinth in my garden is like having an anchor, a walking meditation that is permanently part of this garden's landscape.

As I am writing this, a blue jay is taking a bath in the bird bath. I can see him (her?) throwing water around – a good view from where I am sitting at the dining room table. A statue of St. Francis watches this bath thing silently. Looks more like play time than bath time.

A question – what orients you to where you live?

Part of the appeal of this smaller older home here in Sarasota was the huge rubber tree in the back garden. It was even featured in a video advertising the house for sale.

The tree provides shade all year long. I am grateful.

A rubber tree, as you would expect, yields rubber. When I looked up a photo of a rubber tree, I was surprised to see it doesn't look like my tree.

But my tree does look like the ones I've seen at the Edison & Ford Winter Estates in Fort Myers. I looked up a definition of Ficus and dictionary.com said:

"Any of numerous chiefly tropical trees, shrubs, and vines belonging to the genus Ficus, of the mulberry family, having milky sap and large, thick, or stiff leaves, including the edible fig, the banyan, and many species grown as ornamentals."

There you have it. Ficus. The sap of my tree is milky. Leaves are tick, large and stiff. When they fall to the ground it sounds like mini bombs going off. Kaboom!

My Ficus tree has an agenda. It wants to take over the world. But first – the back garden will do. Roots spread everywhere. Long limbs arch over the house.

I believe my tree and I need to have a talk about boundaries. We had that talk. It did not work. On to Plan B.

What is Plan B? Inviting a friend who owns a chain saw over for a cutting session. That worked.

Gingers are growing along the fence line near the Ficus. I brought a few red cones from Ocala, put them in the ground and they go through a yearly cycle.

Now in October the green leaves are turning yellow. The entire plant dies back. But not to worry, when the rains come in summer, up come the ginger plants again.

Watching all this life cycle is truly amazing to me. My military family never put down roots, staying long enough to see change.

We moved every nine or twelve months. I didn't realize that dying leaves was not the end, only a dormant phase. And who knew Ficus trees wanted to take over the world?

In the center of my garden are some coonties. This is Florida's only native cycad. Cycads are ancient plants often called living fossils – they were around when dinosaurs walked the earth!

In South Florida the atala butterfly lays its eggs on coonties. If these butterflies ever decide to move to southwest Florida, I am ready to welcome them.

These atala caterpillars are on the underside of coontie leaves at Pan's Garden in West Palm Beach, Florida.

Let's start with the aroma of freshly baked bread right out of the oven. Mummmmm, this is down home comfort.

Much needed right now. We don't know who the next president of the United States will be. If it is the same person as the last four years, how can we possibly survive the carnage he will cause?

Staying grounded isn't easy. I asked recently what orients you to where you live. DL answered: "Being in a boat, at dawn or dusk, in a secluded surrounding."

Works for me. I saw a small boat at the Bayfront, downtown Sarasota.

I wanted to find some oars, climb aboard and row away from land, become unmoored, free to follow wind and tide. A daydream (and besides the boat already has an owner). Ah, details.

Meanwhile, as I fret, the front lawn is finally getting some attention from me. Since moving here my focus has been in the back garden – building ponds, making butterfly friendly areas, reducing the grass footprint, creating Mother Nature friendly ecosystems. Just a few projects.

Even while ignoring the front of my house, I can walk around the neighborhood and be full of opinions about other front yards. Easy to make comments, harder to commit to change my front yard. I admit, it is time to lower my carbon footprint in the front and be more inviting to pollinators.

A friend suggested starting by putting a ring of pavers around a tree called a shady lady. The pavers make a container for soil and native plants.

A plan! Try the brand called Jungle Growth available at Lowes. It amends the soil. Yes, gardeners use words like amend. But they are not talking about changing the Constitution. Rather changing the soil – charging it up with new nutrients. Should make the tree happy too.

Rain. So much rain. We are all hunkered down inside.

Bella my dog does not understand how I can expect her to go do her duty in the rain. She gives me an accusing look. This rain is all my fault. I should make it stop. Not happening.

Every dog in my life assumed humans caused the rain to fall.

My three ponds in my back garden are full, close to overflowing. There is standing water on the veranda. Eta, the name of this weather event, has turned into a hurricane.

I used to worry that goldfish would be swept out of ponds to flop around the veranda. But I know better now, after watching them go through heavy rains. Down to the bottom of ponds they go, not to be seen again until the sun comes out.

Yet flowers are blooming even as it rains. The cranberry hibiscus and candlestick cassia are showing their colors.

Cranberry hibiscus are not only beautiful blooms but edible! Gather the pods, even the petals, boil with water – and this makes a lovely red tea, good hot or cold.

Mine are pass along plants and they are taking over a piece of the garden.

Candlestick cassia gets its name as the blooms stand up like candlesticks. This is a host plant for sulphur butterflies.

All this butterfly gardening and ponds and projects takes tools. Here they are.

Not pictured: wheelbarrow – often needed, much appreciated plus electric lawnmower for those patches of grass still left in my back garden.

While the sound of rain is soothing, the national news is anything but. From euphoria last week when Joe Biden was elected President of the United States to fear this week that the former guy plans to blow up the world rather than leave the White House.

These are the words Poynter Institute used to describe our national mood BEFORE the election: Scared. Unsettled. Stressed. Angry. Nerve-racked. Nauseous.

These are the words Poynter Institute is using to describe our national mood AFTER the election: Scared. Unsettled. Stressed. Angry. Nerve-racked. Nauseous.

This is a good time to unplug. Step away from the news. Play with the dog. Read a book. Take a walk when it stops raining.

Or stay plugged in but change the channel. Watch "This Changes Everything" on You Tube.

This is a documentary on climate change. To be the change, get started by watching the video on You Tube by Doug Tallamy called "The little things that run the world – how to create a pollinator backyard."

Today is Veteran's Day. All the menfolk on both sides of my family, until this generation, were career military. Most of the funerals in my life have been at national cemeteries. To this day hearing Taps will reduce me to tears.

I do so wish my dad was alive still, sitting at the family dining room table (now at my home), holding forth on his opinions on the state of the union. My father loved this country. The same cannot be said of the former guy and his followers.

When the past blends into the present we may not even notice unless someone holds up a hand and says – stop, look, learn.

And so, it was an eye-opening experience last Sunday to take the walking tour of the Central Coconut Historic District. I've driven through this area a zillion times and had no idea so many homes were on the National Register of Historic Places.

Such a variety of architectural styles! I added new words to my vocabulary – bungalow, transitional style, modern influence, mission revival, Mediterranean revival, Spanish revival, and Masonry vernacular.

I saw old homes in a new light, seeing the historic significance of 16-pane windows, different rooflines, and influences.

All that and more in under an hour walk. We were socially distanced and masked with ten people tops for each tour. Put on by the Sarasota Alliance for Historic Preservation, our guide was Lorrie Muldowney, a past president of the Alliance.

If there ever was a time to look at the past still living near you in the present, this is it. Why not? No need to get on a plane for new discoveries of old places. Just start exploring, with guides, closer to home.

From natural areas old enough to remember ancient footfalls to historic districts that connect us to the past, these areas are waiting for us to stop, look, learn.

One couple told me they lived two blocks away from where the tour started. They walk their neighborhood every day. And still they learned new things on this tour. Ah, learning new things. How fine is that!

My back garden continues to create its own world. When the new pond was dug, I asked for pass along plants for the edges. Pattie brought some lilies that still thrive near her fifty-year old pond. I planted them. Last week the first bloom opened. Lovely.

The weather event called Eta came last week as a tropical depression then made a rerun as a hurricane. Rain all day and all night. Four inches of rain. Standing water in the garden. Ponds full. Debris everywhere, palm fronds, pine tree branches, Ficus tree branches and zillions of pine needles.

As every gardener knows, it isn't just the raking into piles. All that yard waste, the bits not being recycled in the yard or compost bin, must be hauled to the curb. Ah, the joys of having a back garden. I am not complaining, just whining a bit. That back garden is where I stay grounded (rooted?).

Lately I notice myself lingering on words that can serve as anchors. Words to hold onto in the face of so many question marks in both daily and national life.

Here are three words to ground you every day this week.

This

Here

Now

I'm a sucker for a latte or cappuccino. True confession: I visit local Sarasota coffee shops way too frequently.

When I come through the door, the barista says: The usual?" I nod. This is what happens when you are a regular.

One evening at home I watched a Prime mystery in Italian with subtitles. The lead detective made an expresso and stood by a chateau window. Ah, I remember those small white cups and saucers – that is how expresso is served in France.

There was two-tier pricing. Order an expresso and stand at the bar – one price. Sit and a table and order, another price and this one higher. Cheaper to stand, cup in hand.

Naturally I spent quality time with an elbow on the bar, sipping strong coffee from a small white demitasse cup.

Since Europe is out of the question these days for so many reasons, why not bring Europe here? In the fulness of time, that happened. An expresso machine now graces my kitchen counter along with those small white cups and saucers and a bag of expresso beans.

Took a while to get the hang of making a cappuccino but I've got it down now. Practice makes perfect and the coffee makes my day.

Side benefit – I'm down to one coffee shop visit a week, saving money. Such a small thing to be grateful for – a good cup of coffee.

And I'm grateful for our connection through Wednesday Notes. I asked a while back to draw what you are feeling these days. Here is Anna's reply:

"I can't draw or take photos, but I always have words: Perturbed. Worried. Hopeful. Praying. Confused. Never giving up!!!"

Wonderful! Thank you, Anna. I want a T-shirt with the words NEVER GIVING UP!

Wow. Ceil in Tallahassee took photos of all the landscaping she has done in her back garden and now it is a great place to sit and watch the sunset. Glorious sunsets! Usually, I think of stunning sunsets as happening at the beach, but her photos are taken inland.

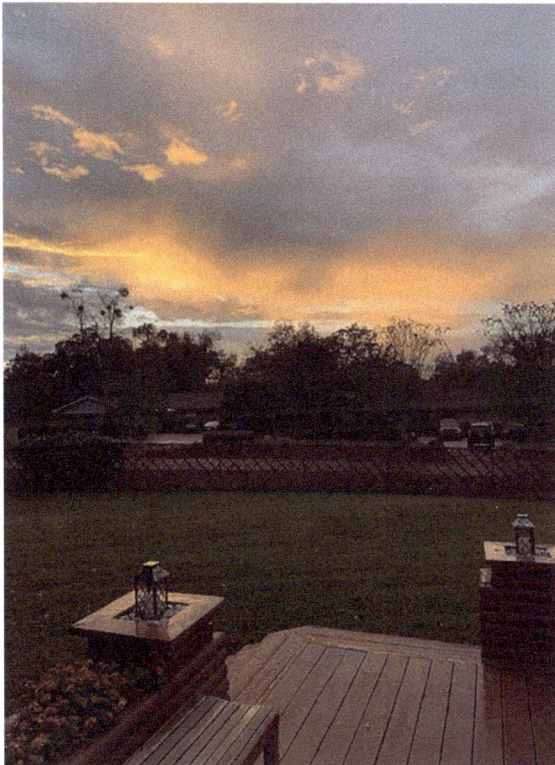

Well, who knows what might be happening with sunsets where you are? Pencil in sunset watching on your calendar.

I hear some Sarasota residents are gathering near the Intracoastal Waterway in the evenings. They bring folding chairs and wine and toast the sunset. This could be a plan!

Moving on from skies to soil, the Sarasota Butterfly Club had a virtual meeting last week where President Karen Rosenbeck  presented a slide show on planting in containers. She introduced words new to me – thrillers, fillers, and spillers.

Thrillers are the tall "wow" flowers planted in the back of a container.

Fillers are those flowers filling up the middle of a container.

Spillers are flowers that trail off and down the front of a container.

Speaking of plants and my admission that I talk to my plants; Edna was prompted to write:

"I also talk to the few inside plants I have but I found that they do even better when I sing to them as I touch their leaves gently. At first, I thought they would die when they heard my singing, but they are strong and alert and probably wondering what the strange noise is."

It has been quite a while since singing in the choir. I too can sing to plants. It will be a strange sound, singing, not heard in these parts for a long time. Thank you, Edna.

Everywhere I turn so far this December I hear stories of traditional Christmas gathering being abandoned. Fears of COVID leading to healthy caution.

But does this mean no guests? Well, think outside the box. Invited feathered friends. Make homemade treats like the old favorite – a pinecone rolled in peanut butter then birdseed and hung on a limb.

Take the family on a pinecone gathering trips. A state park or county park with old pine trees works nicely. Mine came from the ground in my back garden, compliments of the stately pine tree.

Set up containers with sides – one for peanut butter, one for birdseed. Roll a pinecone in peanut butter, get it fully coated, then roll the pinecone in birdseed so it is covered. Have waxed paper or a third container nearby to place the finished pinecones. Tie on a string or bright colored ribbon and hang from a tree limb.

I placed one in the bird feeder and hung several from tree branches. Sit back and enjoy your guests. Yes, squirrels are also attracted to these rolled pinecones. This is a fact of life.

As you have guessed, making pinecone birdfeeders is a messy project. Great for kids. Have paper towels and a bucket of water nearby for cleaning hands.

Simple. Fun. Homemade. No need to order online. You probably did the project once at camp or later with kids and grandkids. What is old becomes new again.

Sometimes it is a good thing to go for a walk in the woods. And so, I went. My destination – Lemon Bay Park and Environmental Center, 570 Bay Park Blvd., Englewood, Florida

The plan – walk at least part of the two-mile long Eagle Trail. Even in the parking lot I could tell the trail was going to be busy. Cars arrived and walkers/runners (easy to tell by their shoes) emerged.

The Eagle Trail comes by its name honestly. Eagles nest in the tall live slash pines.

From the parking lot head for the butterfly garden arbors, turn right, continue onto the trail. I had fun looking up trying to spot eagles or their nests. No joy. But the sky was a full wash of blue, no clouds. The air light and crisp and the shell path meandered leisurely. Inviting turns along the way made me wonder what could be found around the next bend.

I bought a mask just in case and soon had to put it on. People in singles, doubles, groups along with dog walkers kept coming and going. This is a popular trail. Honestly, I should have realized Saturday morning would be prime time.

I felt relaxed. I needed a break from my back garden maintenance. It is a wonderful place, yet I can't look around the garden without mentally making a list of chores.

Here at Lemon Bay, I completely enjoy the moment. Someone else does the maintenance. It is not my problem. I stopped walking and sat on a bench soaking up sun, relishing the fact that nothing is required of me except to be here now.

Give yourself the gift of walking outdoors in the woods if you can. For a short while, step away from Christmas 2020, a scene so tinged with sadness and loss that putting up wreaths and setting out the creche seems like too much effort – at least to me.

I miss my mom. She was my best friend and a good listener who did not judge, just listened, with sympathy, offering much needed advice (not always heeded).

Mom died three days after Christmas long ago. I still have the urge to pick up the phone and dial a very familiar number so we could talk.

Lucy Maude Ord Beebe was first and foremost a California girl, growing up in San Diego. She swam a lot, once training for Olympic tryouts with long swims in the Pacific Ocean. She also desired to grow all things beautiful and always planted flowers wherever we were stationed (my dad was career US Navy).

That DNA must explain why I am a masters swimmer and happiest in my back garden. I miss the flowers that always bloomed around my mom. But she left a legacy.

Being married to a naval officer meant moving a lot. Mom bought California poppy seeds that produce those bright orange blossoms in springtime.

When we'd be driving through faraway places like Idaho and Wyoming my mom rolled down the window and cast seeds into the wind. Five hundred years from now archeologists will try to explain how California poppy seeds ended up blooming in the foothills of Wyoming and Idaho. I could tell them the answer. My mom.

Like many in California who were serious swimmers, mom spent less time in the pool and more time in open water.

One day on a training swim in the Pacific she swam alone (not a good idea) for over a mile straight out from shore. Then leg cramps hit her hard. She tried swimming for shore using only her arm but current and waves kept her in place. She was fading.

Calling for help, she heard no response and saw no one nearby. Then, as if in answer to her call, dolphins (or porpoises?) arrived and surrounded her. One dolphin put a fin under one of her arms. Another dolphin did the same with her other arm.

They gently lifted her up to the top of the water and guided her to shore then swam away when her feet touched the sand.

She would tell this story of the day dolphins saved her life. I am grateful to them. Years later my mom and dad got married and here I am. None of this would have happened without the dolphins.

I too have a dolphin story. Eight years ago, I came to Sarasota from my home in Ocala to attend a travel writers conference. Taking an extra day to write local stories I found myself crossing the John Ringling bridge on a Sunday morning, windows down, inhaling salt air.

Runners and walkers crossed the bridge both ways. Bikers slowly climbed the ascent, making this bridge one of the few hills around Sarasota.

Suddenly I said out loud: "This is where I am supposed to be."

Shocked me. I never saw that coming. And by the way no one else was in the car. Went home to Ocala and told my pastor that story.

He said: "Oh, you have been called.:

"Called to do what?? I asked.

"You will figure it out when you get there," he responded.

I came back to Sarasota to look for a place to live. Sitting in the Bird Key parking lot I dialed the number of a realtor that a friend gave me. As the phone rang, I saw dolphins leap out the water right in front of me.

She answered the phone saying "hello, hello" but I am speechless. Seeing the dolphins, to me, was a sign.

I managed to answer the phone. Liz Nason found me the perfect downsized home. Three months later I moved to Sarasota.

At this time of year, wrapping up what has been both a remarkable and forgettable 2020, remembering mom and significant events. I have to say I am so grateful to be here, near the water, where dolphins leap and new beginnings are possible.

# Winter 2021

New year. New you. The resolution to lose ten pounds in two weeks. Been there. Done that. Or paint the entire house. Way too big a project. None of us could agree on colors for starters.

But wait. You can have a new you in 2021. Just take it gently. I like the suggestion in the New York Times to replace New Year's Resolutions with the words More and Less.

Here is the drill: Use a ruler to draw a big square on a blank sheet of paper. Divide the square in two. Label one side MORE and the other side LESS.

Some of my scribbles:

MORE dancing, talking long walks, singing

LESS looking at social media, watching prime video

No, I won't be dancing with a partner but twirling around the living room by myself. Probably scare the furry ones – a dog and two cats who will duck and cover, not to be seen for some time.

Have fun with this. Use words and drawings.

2021

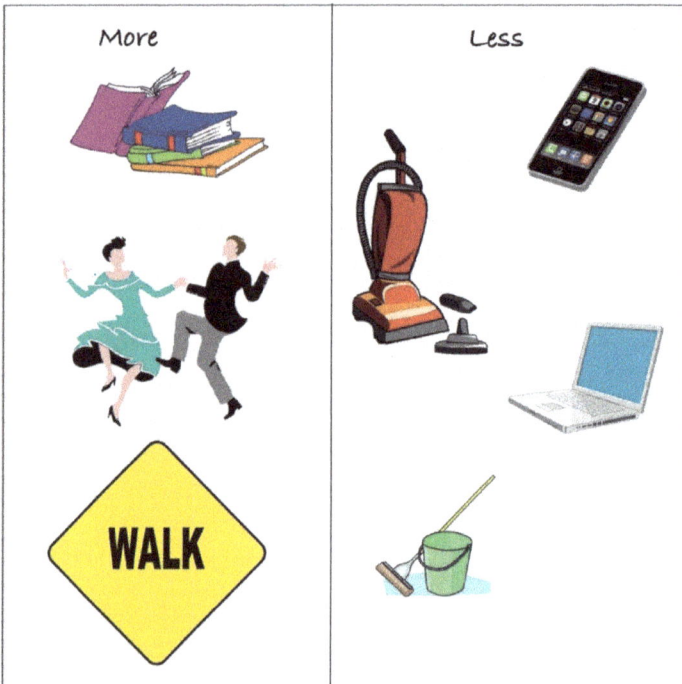

I think the words MORE and LESS are trending since the pandemic went from a short-term detour to a fulltime siege.

MORE time spent outside in the back garden.

LESS time traveling in a car.

MORE time trying new recipes.

LESS time wondering what to wear.

My fish in the outdoor ponds are gone. Disappeared. Nowhere to be found.

I came out recently for morning feeding, tossing pellets into the big pond with five goldfish averaging five inches long and the 120-gallon pond with four fish about the same size.

Not one came to the surface. Not a ripple. Puzzling. No evidence of foul play (like torn up plants, fish parts thrown around on the veranda – typical calling cards left by raccoons).

I even went totally paranoid for a moment or two, wondering if a person had scaled my fence armed with net and bucket and stolen fish. Not happening. Gate closed and locked. Fence six feet tall.

Missing fish. A mystery.

But the culprit just could not stay away. The morning after every fish disappeared, I raised the bedroom window shade and there, standing tall on the veranda, was a great blue heron. Came back to see if there were second servings. The nerve!

Nothing there. But he (or she) came back the following day too just to make sure. I let my dog Bella out. The heron decided to flap its wings, get liftoff, and leave.

Now I have empty fishponds. This is what happens when outdoor ecosystems are created. Life thrives. Pollinators arrive. Predators arrive. Some get eaten. I feel like I am watching and being part of a sitcom like Days of Our Lives.

I miss my morning feeding fish routine.

Speaking of routines – since watching our country be broken last Wednesday as American citizens invaded the U.S. Capitol – I feel powerless, drifting without any meaningful routine.

But then I read a sermon by Dr. Martin Luther King Jr. (his sermons are also on You Tube). In this one King talks about the three dimensions – length, breadth, and width – and translating these dimensions as – love yourself, love others, love God.

How can you love yourself if you feel powerless? If you don't love yourself, how can you help others.

King reminded us that "I am somebody."

I sat up straighter just reading those words. Thank you, Dr. King. I am somebody. I totally lost sight of that while watching homegrown bullies desecrate the Capitol.

Now the blame game begins. Talking heads speak of white discontent, victims who feel disenfranchised.

I respectfully disagree. These are domestic terrorists who ran rampant because they could. And we know who they are. The same bullies, or the children of the same bullies, who in school and the work world hit and belittled people they considered inferior to themselves. Why? Because they could get away with it.

We have met bullies in our lives and may have been their victims. White bullies count on getting a pass because they are white.

But not this time. Lower all American flags to half-mast. Keep them there as our nations goes through a long session of accountability. Destructive actions have consequences.

Then, when justice is served, the perpetrators arrested and sent to prison, raise the flags to full mast and rebuild,

Today I do not feel powerless, and neither should you. You are somebody. You matter. Your actions matter. I know several you are engaged in social justice work – advancing diversity, equity, inclusion, and accessibility.

If you are not engaged in speaking out, making social justice a reality, then get involved. Call your representatives. Tell them exactly how you feel about last Wednesday. Speak up. Your voice matters.

Glorious. That is the word Rick used to describe January 20, 2021 – Inauguration Day. Glorious indeed.

Feels like a great weight has been lifted making it possible to breathe again, to roll up our sleeves and rebuild from the wreckage of four terrible Trump years and the Capitol invasion by domestic terrorists.

A Facebook image of the inauguration invitation circulated with the suggestion – ladies, wear your pearls. And so it came to pass that Gloria and Kate S. both wore their pearls as they watched the amazing day unfold on television.

Mine stayed in the drawer. I can't even remember the last time I wore them. Instead, I wore my Ruth Ginsberg shirt. I know she was there in spirit.

While I do not have television, I do have access to news on the computer. What a great joy to hear Amanda Gorman, Poet Laureate of 2017, read her poem.

Amanda's hands danced as she read. The poem carried the rhythm of a rap song. And rhyming, challenging lyrics lifted the momentous occasion to a higher level.

Her last lines are a call to action:

"The new dawn balloons as we free it,

For there is always light, if only we are brave enough to see it.

If only we're brave enough to be it."

Amen.

In addition to glorious, amazing is my second word of the week. Last week a great blue heron ate all the goldfish out of my ponds, or so I thought.

Turns out two fish survived! I was using a pond net to scoop out Ficus leaves in the big pond and saw something orange way down at the deep end underneath a bog plant.

I realized it was a goldfish, not moving, When I tried to scoop it up, the fish moved just slightly. Also uncovered another one in deep hiding. These are severely traumatized fish. They do not come to the surface for food. But when I come back later, the food pellets are gone.

Three cheers for the survivors! I hope the fish shelter, still on backorder, comes soon so they can have someplace to hide besides mud.

Once there were nine goldfish in my big pond. Then a murderous raid by a great blue heron two weeks ago reduced that number to two. The remaining fish hid in the deep end of the pond under the roots of a water plant. Can you blame them?

And I am not the only one getting heron visits. Susan, a neighbor, says she too has a heron checking out her fishponds. That bird is making the rounds and taking the concept of dining out to a whole new level.

I've been asked if new fish will appear. Yes. But first I've ordered koi castles, fancy words for mini-Quonset huts, 13 inches long and six inches high. These sit on the bottom and provide a shelter (hiding place) for fish. The huts are on backorder. Must be a lot of fish feeling threatened out there.

Could be because a lot of folks are building new ponds during these pandemic times. New ponds = new opportunities for marauders like raccoons, otters, blue herons, and great white egrets.

Two new water lilies grace the big pond. Arrowroot plants are ordered and on the way. I'm looking for pickerel plants. Any suggestions?

     All that foliage makes it difficult for a wading bird to wade around in the pond.

     While the ponds have water, a lack of rain has made it imperative to keep the bird baths full. And I've added more bird baths as the birds are looking for water.

Sitting at the dining room table I looked out at the veranda. Two mourning doves sat in a bird bath. A St. Francis statue next to the bird bath kept watch.

Was St. Francis of Assisi thinking the same as me – why are two birds sitting in the bird bath? Not taking a bath or having a drink. Just sitting in the water. It is never dull in the back garden. Something new going on every day.

Perhaps it is the long pandemic confinement. Or the loss of everyday order (where did normal go?). Even a fear of chaos that could occur without a compass. Whatever the reason I have a newfound fascination with patterns.

Patterns are guides. Repetitions that carry weight. Patterns are comforting. Seen any good patterns lately? Do share.

Happy early Valentine's Day. Original illustration by Lucy Tobias ©2021 and yes, it was fun to make the PATTERNS. Share love – be love – love yourself.

Don't believe the calendar. Just because the almanac calls for spring to arrive on Saturday, March 20, that does not make it so.

Trust your senses. Feel the soft caress of a warm breeze on your arms and face. Smell the slight perfume of blooming flowers. These things are the siren songs of spring. The songs of spring may be brief and revert to winter again, but while it lasts it is real.

My back garden is already making spring music. Flowers wave their blossoms in a gentle breeze, inviting me to sink into the chaise lounge and inhale the smell of spring.

A stalk of Mexican sunflowers growing next to the St. Francis statue has burst forth with total exuberant blooms. In the nearby big pond, the new water lily sends up a bloom that leans towards the east to catch the rising morning sun.

Under a bird feeder blooms a blanket flower. I bought a blanket flower plant two years from the native plant nursery at the Edison and Ford Winter Estates in Fort Myers. Wonderful nursery. You will not go home empty handed. I highly recommend a visit.

And why should all the flowers stay outside? Bring in nasturtium blooms, they are edible, and decorate salads or grilled vegetables. Yum.

Don't have nasturtiums? Consider checking out local sources. Mine came from Homestead Hydroponics. Order from them online and pick up on a designated day. Hydroponic farms are a good source for organic produce and things like nasturtiums.

I have planted nasturtium seeds and hope to have my own flowers later in the spring or early summer. Nasturtium blooms taste a bit like lemon pepper.

Today is Ash Wednesday, the start of forty days of Lent. When I was growing up, Lent meant we had fish for dinner on Fridays.

My dad was Methodist, but he got into the Catholic spirit of things during Lent. At one point we were living in Washington D.C. and my dad (career Navy) was stationed at the Pentagon.

He learned the local Howard Johnson's restaurant (remember them?) had an all you can eat fish fry during Lent, serving catfish caught locally in the Potomac. Probably not the best environmental choice but still, off we went every Friday.

I was, at the age of nine, indifferent to the fish fry but quite enthusiastic about their 31 flavors of ice cream.

Ah, yesterdays. For today and this year's season of Lent, consider something radical – adding Meatless Mondays to your calendar.

Means less resources like water and grain wasted on raising beef. Think of Meatless Mondays as not a giving up of something but a step forward to more sustainable living.

To know more how eating, especially beef, affects our footprint on Mother Earth, visit Foodprint.org

Meanwhile, this Lent, I'll be looking for a fish fry on Fridays.

A thank you to Judy for these parting thoughts:

Celebrate your days.

Cherish your memories.

Last week a morning stroll around my back garden produced a panic moment.

Looking at the big pond I saw something very out of place – a monarch caterpillar on a lily pad. Blown there by the wind? Who knows?

It was one of those "am I seeing what I think I'm seeing?" moments. I froze.

The caterpillar came to the edge of the lily pad and put some of its many feet into the water. Panic time for me. Drowning time for the caterpillar.

DO SOMETHING RIGHT NOW.

I looked around, saw a small clay pot, grabbed it. Slid the pot under the lily pad leaf and caterpillar and scooped all of it out of the pond.

Then the pot and I took a walk around the garden. I'm looking for milkweed (a monarch's host plant). Found one in the side yard. Put the wet caterpillar on a milkweed leaf and munching started immediately.

Drowning averted. Happy ending. Whew!

Drama in the back garden – a real life soap opera.

The word for today is . . . perseverance.

Used as in NASA's Perseverance and the seven minutes of terror as it made a perfect landing on Mars. I do not have television but can get it all on news videos.

Think of the task – traveling 300 million miles, slowing down for a fiery atmospheric entry, firing eight retrorockets, then using nylon cords to put the 2,300-pound rover on the surface. And it worked. Congratulations to the National Aeronautics and Space Administration.

This feat makes my brain cells fire off randomly, overloaded with the sheer immensity of scientific knowledge plus teamwork to make this landing possible. I have heard that eighty six percent of the Mars team are women. Yes!

And here is a shout out for more science education. Science is important.

Having solved landing on Mars, could the Mars team turn to tackle some earth problems like the totally chaotic vaccine distribution system – and turn it into a working machine?

One friend suggested if women oversaw delivering the vaccines it would be done by now. Just saying.

For those who missed it, the rover parachute used in the Mars mission contained a hidden message. The unusual red and white design inside the canopy turns out to be binary code ( I didn't figure it out by myself, Internet sleuths did).

When translated it reads:

"Dare mighty things."

The words come from a speech by Theodore Roosevelt in 1899.

Dare mighty things. Words for our time.

Every spring an artworks exhibit takes shape outdoors at Bayfront Park in downtown Sarasota, Florida. It is called Embracing our Differences.

If there ever was a time we need to embrace our differences, that time is now.

Artists from all over the world submit artwork. Students write verses. Sponsors spring for the billboard size artworks that are chosen.

Here are the 2021 numbers: 15,912 entries from 128 countries and 48 states and 412 are pieces of school artwork or quotes.

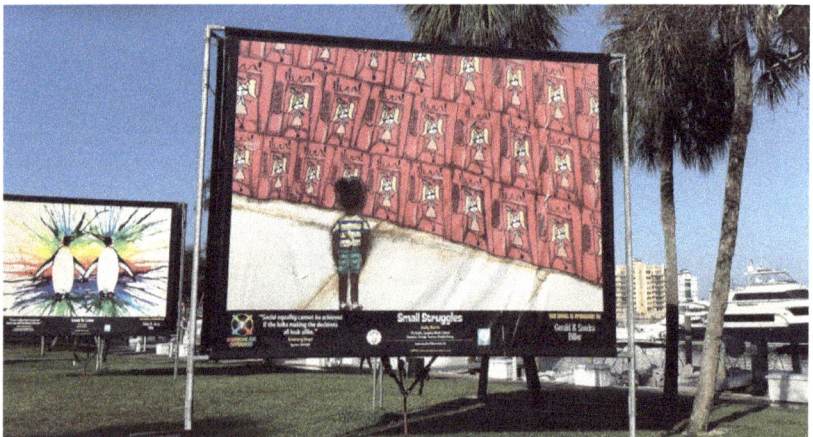

The best in show is a billboard by Emily N., a 7th grader at Sarasota Middle. It shows a young black girl standing in front of a store display of dolls. All the dolls are white. The title is Small Struggles to reflect the small struggles people of color go through every day.

A billboard that caught my attention is entitled Unity. The artist is Evelyn Homewood, a 12th grader at Stratford Girls Grammar School in Royal Leamington Spa, United Kingdom.

On the left is a classic Greek goddess. The assumption is she is white. On the right is a Nigerian princess, every bit a goddess. Perception is everything. Behind both is a classic Renaissance cloud cover.

An accompanying quote reads: "An oppressive society forces its citizens to be the same. An empowering society protects its citizens' right to be different."

The author of this quote is Sarah S., a 12th grade student at Henry M. Gunn High School, Palo Alto, California.

Added pluses – as you wander around the park reading billboards you also get to see the beautiful Bayfront, moored boats, the tall arch of the John Ringling bridge and perhaps pelicans diving for fish in the Intracoastal Waterway.

There are benches for sitting and indulging in morning meditation. Dog walkers strut by. Mothers push baby carriages as they put in their jogging miles.

The exhibit is all outside. There is no charge. Embracing our Differences stays up until April 1.

Am I trying to get you outside! Yes.

If you have been housebound because of COVID 19 fears (rightly so) let me point out that spring has sprung even though it is officially still winter. Welcome to Florida where the weather and season change in a nanosecond.

It is warmer than it was a month ago. Flowers are blooming. Go outdoors. Bring a mask. Stay socially distanced.

Being outdoors is good for your physical, mental, and emotional health.

Pack away your fear along with your winter clothes. Put a lid on to box. Step out into springtime.

Ah, springtime.

I've always loved the start of an e.e.cummings poem:

"sweet spring is your time, is my time, is our time . . ."

You might have noticed no capitals, that is because e.e.cummings did not like capitals!

148

For a finale today let us look at the billboard by Best in Show Adult – Liberty Enlightening the World by Arya Badiyan of Lake Oswego, Oregon.

Lady Liberty is a Black woman, and the artist reminds us that the original statue of liberty design carried chains in her hands to reflect the emancipation of Black people. Later, those chains were placed on her feet,

The many faces depicted behind her show millions of Black lives lost to injustice and slavery in the United States.

An accompanying quote by Seth Morano, Sarasota, Florida reads:

"Don't wait for better leaders, become one."

Raise your hand if you recognize this tool and know what to do with it.

Ah. Good. You got it. A squeegee – used for wiping windows.

Which leads to a Mother Earth moment. Ditch commercial window cleaners. They are toxic. Instead, mix up a batch of water and vinegar, fifty-fifty mix, or water and rubbing alcohol. Put in a spray bottle or wipe the window with clean cloth and solution. Finish with the squeegee. My, what a difference clean windows make! The view improves. And so does your mood. Go for it.

Speaking of going for it – a round of applause please for Serenaty Lumpkin, a junior in high school, who just published her first book – a book of her poems.

I have been doing informal mentoring with Serenaty for several years. We talk about writing poetry, style, content and then, since her goal was a book, we worked towards doing just that.

Should you be a Sarasota Downtown Farmers Market regular, you already know her family. Her grandmother is the French crepe maker. Often a daughter and grandchild (Serenaty) help. Our mentoring sessions were often done with a crepe in hand.

Serenaty has many mentors – proof that we are all walking this journey of life together, sharing knowledge, questions, answers. I am honored to be a small part of her walk.

Her book title is *Asterism – Collection of Poems Vol. 1* available on Amazon as paperback or Kindle. It is 278 pages.

Serenaty's short poems can often strike me as lightbulb moments. Here is one:

"Perhaps it is not our hearts that
Long to be held, but our soul
When we feel alone."

©swl2020

And sometimes her poems make me laugh out loud:

"So much work, so much

Stress

I do not like it, I must

Confess."

©swl2020

There is even a section of international poems translated into different languages. Ah, I must confess I am envious. There are so many opportunities for emerging writers today.

Serenaty started think about a book more than a year ago. She wanted a book to show college recruiters in her junior year. The way to go – self-publishing.

That was never an option in my day. Traditional publishers only. Took years to establish enough credentials that they would even look at your work (still true today). Audio books were rare. Self-publishing did not exist.

Serenaty had a book signing at the market last weekend. Congratulations! On the back flap of her book, she summarizes why she writes:

"We write to free ourselves from ourselves.

We write to be remembered.

We write to calm our minds.

We write to live."


Amen. I could not have said it better. And now it is your turn – find a blank piece of paper and write a poem. Go for it.

Sure and begorrah we are all Irish today, St. Patrick's Day. Wear green. Ah, I could find nothing green in the closet. I settled for shades of green from the garden.

A succulent with a subtle shade of green. The suggestive green of clover. A wild coffee plant with bright green shiny leaves.

Mother Nature thanks all of you who resonated with my plea to use water and vinegar or water and rubbing alcohol instead of commercial toxic window cleaners.

Anna, who grew up in Brooklyn, said:

"By the way my family washed windows ONLY with vinegar and water. It kept the dust, dirt, and grease of the city from sticking on the glass."

In garden circles where pollinators are important, the current mantra is: Bring on the insects (pollinators) and the birds will follow.

Easy to say but the reality can be a bit shocking.

One morning while sitting outside near the big pond, I watched a bee collecting pollen on Spanish needles, going from one flower to another. Impressive how busy he was. So many flowers, so little time.

Indeed. So little time turned out to be true. A mockingbird swooped down right in front of me, grabbed the bee, swallowed it whole and flew away.

Bam! One minute live and buzzing. Next moment dead and gone. Shocking really. I sat there stunned.

Tough to witness but this is exactly what the cycle of life is about. Eighty percent of a bird's diet is insects. Especially important when nesting as they bring insects to the young for meals.

Ecological author Doug Tallamy talks about how certain species provide more services than others.

Services. That bee, unintentionally, provided a service to the bird. Easy to talk the environmental talk – bring on the pollinators – not so easy to walk the walk in real life – watch a pollinator get eaten.

If you spend any time outdoors watching Mother Nature do her wildlife thing you are familiar with the eat or be eaten concept.

Despite the shock I'll be planting more flowers to attract more pollinators to bring more birds. The cycle continues.

Two Tallamy books I recommend: *Nature's Best Hope* (2009) and *Bringing Nature Home: How You Can Sustain Wildlife with Native Plants* (2020).

I am still smiling over shades of green from St. Patrick's Day last week. Thus, it is fitting as we get ready to walk the walk today to end with the Irish blessing which is also a prayer:

May the road rise to meet you.

May the wind be always at your back.

May the sun shine warm upon your face:

The rains fall soft upon your fields and until we meet again,

May God hold you in the palm of his hand.

As a newspaper reporter for the New York Times Group, I worked long unpredictable hours.

Weekends could be long too but often for a different reason. Spring, summer, fall and winter I turned into a nomad, often packing everything up for a weekend art show of my photographs. I set up a tent and led forth as combination artist and performer for two days.

Other exhibitors arrived with their big vans, trailers and SUVs and they all laughed at me. I arrived in small Honda Civic with a rack on top.

The rack held all my display panels. Somehow, in that little car, I stuffed my tent, folding tables, boxes of photographs, even a lunch bag.

Their laughter stopped and amazement started when it all came together. Up went the tent, in went the display panels, photographs hung, tables set up with print bins. Finally, I put on my funky artist's hat and set out my water bottle. Ready for customers.

As the day progressed, I could not help but notice people's attitudes. A lot of passive aggressive action going on between couples. Silent and not so silent tug of war using body language – all about who was in charge.

One example: a woman browsed through my print bin. Her husband, taller and broader, stood behind her, arms folded, looking bored. He could care less that she was interested in the photos.

I got the impression he could care less what she thought about anything. He refolded his arms, stuck out his chest, looking intimidating, making it clear with body language he wanted to leave.

She ignored him.

Finally, it was too much for her. Without saying a word, she turned to leave my booth. He trailed behind.

Wow. Talk about passive aggressive. At that moment, it is embarrassing to say this, but I honestly felt relieved to be divorced so I did not have to live with this kind of behavior.

An hour or so passed.

Suddenly, I see the same woman walking rapidly towards my tent. She is alone.

With total bluntness I asked her:

"Well, what did you do with him?"

She replied:

"I bought him one of those big funnel cakes. He is sitting at a table eating it. I have a few minutes."

I laughed, admiring her creativity.

She went through the bin, picked her favorites, and bought them.

If it takes a funnel cake to make a few moments for yourself, so be it!

As more shows filled my calendar, I turned to a fascination with watching feet go by, the shoes people wore, or didn't wear, and how they walked.

I would try to guess occupations from shoes and walking patterns.

Expensive running shoes with little wear and tear combined with a short stride with no push off must be a weekend warrior showing off the shoe brand. Flash but no dash.

Cleated shoes, spandex pants, tight shirt – there is bike chained nearby.

Worn sandals, old clothes, and a casual stride – this person is comfortable with themselves. No need to impress.

Shoes that matched clothes and jewelry – that person spent time in front of a mirror. Visiting the show is a side detour. They probably have a lunch date.

You get the idea. It was fun. Those show days are gone. So is the tent and display panels, all sold.

Currently, my traveling gear is a box of books I've authored and a jump drive with PowerPoint presentation preloaded. Perhaps a projector and computer, but most often those are already at my destination. I'm ready to talk to groups.

Much smaller footprint, it all fits in my small car, this time a Honda Fit. Throw in a folding table, a tablecloth and chair and I'm equipped to share a tent with another author at craft fairs and book events.

This past year with COVID19 there have been zero events. Just two weeks ago I finally ventured forth for an outdoor event at Five Points, a small, shaded park in downtown Sarasota.

How wonderful to be back live with real people, almost all masked, and all glad to be out and about.

It energized me to talk with people live, to connect. And these real people also bought my books and cards. Bless them all. This time I was inspired to check out people with dogs. There was a surprisingly large number of them walking through the park.

Women wearing high heels and spandex tights favored small dogs with jeweled collars.

Men in weekend casual clothes walked side by side with big dogs like Golden Retrievers sporting leather collars and wagging tails.

Puppies did what puppies do. No attention to their leashes, darting from side to side, convinced everyone passing by is their newest best friend.

Throw in the fact it was a beautiful spring day. A day to see and be seen. A day to be out and about. A great day for dogs and their owners. Seeing them made my day.

I have read that over time dog owners and their dogs start looking alike. Could it be true?

I looked for similarities between dogs and owners. The closest I came was a casually dressed guy with his Golden Retriever. They looked very comfortable with each other. In fact, they looked alike.

So here we go, me and Bella, my rescue dog. Look alike? Not yet. She needs to work on her wrinkles.

And now you know the story behind the story of art and craft shows.

# Spring 2021

Let's talk about poop. Not yours! Not mine! Whew. That is a relief. Caterpillar poop to be exact.

Caterpillar poop has its own name – frass.

Caterpillars eat and poop, eat and poop. The time comes when a caterpillar is full and fat, ready to move onto the next stage of life – turning into a chrysalis. But first a caterpillar moves away, far away as possible, from where it has been eating and pooping.

Why move so far away? In part because of all that frass left behind. Their poop, dropped down below where they ate leaves, has a smell (sound familiar?) that attracts predators that would gladly eat a caterpillar or even chomp on a chrysalis.

I read an article about caterpillars someplace in South America. They are so abundant on a tree that when a biologist came by, he thought it was raining under the tree – all those black things falling on the forest floor. Frass! Full of nutrients. Excellent fertilizer.

Anyone who has raised caterpillars in an enclosed environment knows all about frass that needs to be cleaned out of the enclosure.

Then the marvelous time comes when a green monarch chrysalis turns black, then clear, and finally a fully formed beautiful monarch butterfly emerges from its embryo.

Now it sits still for quite a while, drying its wings, getting ready to fly onto a new life.

Yes, it is easy to title this edition of Wednesday Notes –
The Monarch Chronicles. But the story is bigger than one
species of butterfly. I sit outside and see cloudless sulphur,
yellow butterflies fluttering around cassia plants, put there just
for them.

A great southern white butterfly flits around looking for
a host plant like nasturtiums. I try telling it to come back again,
please, my nasturtiums are just coming up – leaves but no
flowers yet.

Pipevine hangs heavy on the back fence, laden with huge
orchid like flowers. The swallowtails have yet to arrive –
pipevine is a host plant for them.

I see zebra Longwings and gulf fritillaries doing loop de
loops around the garden. Perhaps they can smell their host plant,
passion vine, but are having trouble finding it. That is because
all my passion vine is eaten down to the stems, very few leaves
left. Hopefully, I'll get more plants.

And so it goes. A cycle of eat and poop, eat and deplete
plants. Butterflies looking for nectar and host plants, laying
eggs, doing this cycle over and over.

Their life cycle is part of the rhythm of my days.

And how is the tempo of your days?

These are the in between times. In between the old normal (before COVID19) and the new normal (yet unnamed).

Here, in the in between, we are supposed to reverberate in the moment. That is much easier said than done.

Our minds and hearts easily detach from the moment, flying up and away like a balloon untied from a railing and caught by the morning breeze, drifting over the trees on an uncharted zigzag course headed for sky.

Set free, we dream of tomorrows and drift back to memories of yesterdays. I am not immune to dreams or drifting back.

Not that I want to write a memoir. I'd need a shovel to dig up all the bodies. And yet memories keep floating up.

Here are some from my days as a newspaper reporter. File the following story under BELIEVE IT OR NOT.

I was a newly minted police reporter in Fernandina Beach at a weekly paper owned by the New York Times Regional Group.

Already I was the county beat reporter and the features reporter – this was one more layer. You get the idea. Small staff means the same heads wear many hats while only getting paid to wear one hat.

I thought, how hard could police reporting be?

Ah, I was so naïve.

Off I go on Monday morning to get crime reports from both the city police department and the county sheriff's office. But I ran right into a wall of resistance at least three feet thick and nine feet high.

There is this pesky thing called the Florida Open Records law. Any public agency needs to have its records available for inspection.

I found out quickly there is a price of admission. The gatekeeper of the county records, for example, was a seasoned officer clearly delighted to have fresh media meat.

When I asked for the weekly reports, he stonewalled me, not answering but instead asking if I like the Gators football team. I hedged.

Lucky for me, back at the office, the sports editor's desk was right next to mine. I could care less about football (please forgive me), but I was up to speed as he always had stories from attending games.

I fumbled around, throwing out what little I knew. The gatekeeper smiled a very thin smile. Not a great performance on my part but enough to make a passing grade.

He reached behind him and lifted a fat folder. "The reports," he said. "Desk is over there."

And so, it began.

Every Monday I'd arrive and ask him "How about them Gators?" or other teams it turns out he liked. We'd converse for a few minutes. Niceties observed, the price of admission paid, he would hand over the fat folder.

The drill reminded me of connecting with my dad years before. I was married with small children and living 3,000 miles away from my dad. I looked for ways to stay bonded.

Dad was a big fan of quarterback Joe Montana and the San Francisco 49ers. He watched every game on television. I too watched the games on TV.

On Monday morning I'd call him and say:

"How about those 49ers?"

My dad would be off and running with commentary. I would hold the landline phone next to my ear, smiling. We were connected. That was the point. Even if it meant getting out of my comfort zone and watching football.

Come summer the newspaper hosted an intern for six weeks – a college student majoring in journalism. She walked in the door, head high, knowing it all.

I was tasked to give her assignments. So, I sent her off on Monday morning to get reports form the sheriff's office. I know, it was cruel. But even journalism majors with straight As must experience real life sooner or later.

Real life involves getting over yourself and what you think you know. Instead, listen, pay attention to what is happening around you. This makes all the difference.

An hour later she came back foaming at the mouth, spitting mad. The deputy had flat out refused to give her the crime reports when she asked for them.

She loudly and repeatedly reminded him of the state's open records law. He was unmoved.

I suggested perhaps instead of starting with demands another tact would be to introduce herself, say something about the trip out to the office (long), the weather (hot), being new (translates into 'help me, I'm clueless'), anything to start a conversation. Maybe even find out a little bit about him before making demands.

She snorted in disbelief at my suggestions. How medieval! How old fashioned!

He was a chauvinistic pig! She was a modern, liberated woman (and by default I was not) and she was not about to engage in warmup conversation. It was demeaning.

Well, darlin', good luck with that attitude.

Here is a fact of life – we live below the Mason-Dixon Line. Southern hospitality demands warmup conversation before getting down to business.

When two Southerners meet for the first time there is a whole protocol for establishing connections, for warming up.

Ground to be covered includes – who's your daddy? Who's your mommy? Where is your family from? What church do you attend? What part of town do you live in? Where did you go to college? High school? What is your occupation? Do you volunteer anywhere? Sports played or watched? Where do your kids go to school? Do you sing in the choir?

It is all about establishing bona fides. From then on you are expected to remember connections and ask about them at the next meeting – like an uncle who had surgery, how is he doing? Or a new granddaughter, is she sleeping through the night? Or a football game score, how about them Gators?

About that intern – she refused to go out to the sheriff's office ever again. Her loss.

One day later that fall, long after the intern was gone, I was reading reports at the sheriff's office. A female deputy came into the room. She stood next to the desk, looked around to see if anyone was nearby.

Then she bent down and whispered in my ear:

"Have you ever wondered why there are no child abuse reports?"

Without waiting for an answer, she quickly moved away.

Uh, no. I never wondered. I was too busy reading the reports in front of me every week.

Like the farmer who killed his wife then plowed her under in the fields during spring planting. Or the fatal crash where a husband in his car chased after an estranged wife and her lover in their car. The wife's car totaled into a tree. He drove on.

Then there were the home invasions, robberies, drunk driving, domestic disturbances, shots fired, dogs biting people, drag racing, bar fights – the usual.

But never, not once, did I consider WHAT WAS NOT THERE.

Her words took my breath away. With my editor totally on board I began going to the Nassau County Courthouse a lot, pulling all the crime reports filed for the past year. These were paper reports, before everything went digital.

I would probably do the same thing today as I trust paper reports (assuming a report was made at all) more than the digital versions, which can be easily edited (read stuff deleted). A paper trail is always good.

So many reports. A friend came to help. It took us weeks to read one year, looking for any child abuse reports. We found over 100 – the exact numbers elude me now. That was mind boggling. We did another year, again over 100 cases.

In the end, the child abuse story became a multi-part series in the newspaper. Shock waves ran through the community.

The sheriff said he ordered child abuse reports pulled because it made the county look bad. But keeping things silent so long, and violating the open records law really made everything worse when it all came out.

The other place I had to visit each week was the city police department. This was a different kettle of fish. From day one I would be given one or two reports by the police officer at the front desk and told the chief had to authorize me to see any more.

Humm. Difficult. I can do difficult. I made an appointment to see the chief. We had not previously met. He spent most of his time in his office.

My plan was to remind him, calmly, rationally, of the open records law. That was the only arrow in my quiver.

I had heard through the grapevine that the chief, who had served in the military before becoming a police officer, was ill and might retire at any time.

But that was only a rumor. I knew no facts.

At the appointed day and hour, I knocked on his door.

A male voice said: "Come in."

He was seated behind his desk at the end of the room. He did not look at me or speak. His eyes were fixed on the wall just inside the door.

I entered, shut the door, walked across the room, turned the chair around in front of his desk so it faced the wall. I sat down.

I stared at the wall and saw nothing, just a wall.

"They are coming," the chief said quietly.

Immediately I sat up straighter. Forget seeing things – it was time to listen, smell, maybe even feel whatever the heck was going on here.

Then I heard hoofbeats way off in the distance. Not just one horse but several. They were cantering, moving fast.

"I hear them," I whispered.

The chief nodded.

We sat in silence, looking at the wall, listening.

I grew up in the military. My dad was a career Naval officer. Other family members were career Army or Air Force.

Hence, I knew the story of the Four Horseman of the Apocalypse – conquest or pestilence on a white horse, war on a red horse, famine on a black horse, and death on a pale horse.

They might arrive in visions – most often when death is close by. For example, when wars are going on, men fighting dying. Soldiers heard hoofbeats, sometimes saw riders, all four horsemen.

Those soldiers who were spared, whose time had not yet come, lived to tell the tale of what they saw and heard.

The hoofbeats got louder. They were coming closer.

The two of us sat still and silent as stones.

Eventually I stood up, walked to the door, and turned around to see him still sitting at his desk, still staring at the wall.

I quietly shut the door and left the building.

Later that afternoon the chief called the front desk and said I could have all the reports every week, no need to ask him

He died a few weeks later of stage four cancer.

For me, it was an honor and a privilege to hold vigil with him, however briefly.

I've never uttered a whisper of that encounter to anyone.

Until now.

Looking at the calendar – so many days with special names – hard to keep up. Here are a few:

Plant a Flower Day – March 12

Groundhog Day – February 2

National Arbor Day – April 30

St. Francis of Assisi Feast Day – October 4

National Make a Friend Day – February 11

Earth Day 2021 – April 22, tomorrow

Earth Day was first celebrated in 1970. It feels like we need to go to confession and get absolved of our sins BEFORE we celebrate Earth Day.

Confess that we do not always turn the water off while brushing our teeth. Confess we have forgotten our resolve not to use plastic. Confess that our relationship with Mother Earth has been rocky to say the least.

Never fear. Here is your penitence – five ways to mend your relationship with Mother Earth starting right now.

Ditch the drive through coffee and fast food lanes. Why? $CO_2$ emissions. The more you sit in line with the car running the more air is polluted. Suggestion: Park. Go inside. Or consider going to local coffee shops rather than drive throughs. Crowds are less. Parking is easier.

Reuse coffee grounds for those who are coffee drinkers. One idea: make coffee grounds part of a facial scrub. Ah, homemade scrubs. I did one once that involved oatmeal and yogurt. Mixed up the paste, applied liberally to my face. Let dry. Then the doorbell rang. You can stop laughing now. I can hear you all the way over here.

Cease and desist buying plastic bottles of water. Now. Today. End the practice. And don't feel righteous about buying water in plastic bottles then recycling the bottles. Less than five percent of all those bottles get recycled. The rest end up in landfills and oceans. Stop. Doing. This. Instead buy several stainless steel or ceramic containers. Refill. Keep in refrigerator. Ready to go. And should you need to be reminded. Yes, your buying habits, good or bad, make a difference.

Turn off the water while brushing your teeth. Just a reminder.

Plant a tree. Trees purify the air, combat climate change, provide housing for wildlife big and small, provide shade. Sit under a tree. Meditate. Thank you for every tree and flower you plant or have planted. Love Mother Earth, our beautiful blue orb floating in the Milky Way. It is the only home we have.

The huts have arrived Send up a cheer! Hip! Hip! Hurrah!

They are called koi castles, a place for fish to hide, but to me they look like mini Quonset huts – 13 inches long, 6 inches high.

Why have these huts ? Well, that is a grim story. Four months ago, an American Egret (also known as a Great White Egret) came for a visit and ate all my goldfish.

Then that same bird had the nerve to return the next day looking for seconds.

Something had to be done. The half concrete blocks with their openings that I'd out in the ponds were not enough shelter. So out went an order to The Pond Guy for huts.

But the pandemic has caused serious supply line disruption including my huts on back order month after month.

Finally, an email from the Pond Guy saying the koi castles have arrived and do I still want them? Yes. And now they are installed. Live long and proper all you fish – and may you realize what the hut is for right away.

A few feet away from the ponds a new path project is underway. This path will eventually go all the way around the center of my garden.

But these days I need all the positive reinforcement I can get, and I need it now. So, for this path some six feet or so get finished before moving on. Looks great. Works for me. Positive reinforcement is a powerful tool.

Every Wednesday there is a church Zoom meeting called Sacred Conversation on Race. We gather to understand and hopefully implement racial equality. It is not an easy task.

Felix and Nancy contributed this short piece written by their daughter Lia McElroy Stallworth:

"Have you ever had a paper cut? No big deal. Right? It might sting a little, irritate you, be slightly distracting, but soon you'd forget about it. Imagine if one day you had 10 paper cuts. Or 20?

Does that pain start to accumulate? Would it throb? It damn sure would have your attention. Now imagine someone else is causing these smallish cuts. Every day you receive 10+ small cuts.

Sone days the cuts are tiny like paper cuts and sometimes they are stab wounds. Yet, every day you receive these cuts. Days turn into weeks. Weeks into months, months into years.

Now how ya doing? Are you sensitive? Hurting? Wishing it would end? This is the Black experience. Microaggressions and racist remarks are like paper cuts. Some days they are manageable. Over time they take their toll, and we never get a break.

So, watch what you say. Be aware that it's happening, and if you had to endure a lifetime of daily paper cuts, you'd be tired, too."

Parting thoughts: take a deep breath before saying your next sentence. Be positive reinforcement for someone today.

The new path that will circle the center of my garden continues to happen but not without hiccups.

I frequent Total Landscape Supply in Sarasota that sells wholesale to the trade. They give backyard gardeners like me the same wholesale prices. Here is part of this week's conversation at Total Landscape Supply:

May I have a bag of topsoil?

"No. We are out of topsoil."

How about a bag of potting soil?

"No. We are out of potting soil."

Humm. I get the sense "NO'' is a trending word.

Maybe a bag or two of small brown river rock?

He checks river rock on the computer.

"We have seven bags left."

I bought them all.

And so it goes, one path section at a time – each section in a sequence. Make a trench for the edging using the edger tool. Put in edging cut to length. Dig up grass growing on the path. Rake level. Put in pavers a measured distance apart. Level pavers. Pour bags of river rock around each paver. Buy more supplies. Repeat as needed. Get stopped every few feet to dig out serious rubber tree roots trying to take over the garden.

Gardeners and DIYers who have dug a path before will recognize I am not doing this path the standard way. That involves digging out a path width, removing all vegetation, installing edging, putting down a fist layer of sand then one or two layers of weed barrier cloth, followed by pavers and river rock.

Been there. Done that. It doesn't work. Truth be told all the barriers – sand, weed barrier cloth, do not work. Mother Nature has other plans. Little green things find their way through all those barriers and rise in all their green glory. Pluck them out regularly or live with them.

Since regular maintenance is not part of my life plan if I can avoid it, I've learned to live with the little dears.

But I digress.

The big news involves baby birds taking their first flight. Fledglings! And we (my dog Bella and I) saw it happen LIVE.

While sipping morning coffee and sitting comfortably with Bella on the veranda chaise longue, I could not help but notice Mr. and Ms. Cardinal nearby. They zoomed back and forth across the garden, flying low to the ground, over and over, intense, and focused.

Then a small, fat puffball of a baby bird jumped off the old tree stump in the center of the garden, flapping its wings, gaining a little altitude but losing it fast and plopping down on the ground.

In true helicopter style (that would be parents who hover over their kids) both parents fluttered around the baby bird, clearly concerned, flapping wings, seeming saying: Are you all right? Can you do it again?

Then a second fat puffball of a baby bird took wing. More helicopter parenting.

And we were there! Oh, so exciting. A first.

I want to give a shout out to Liz Nason, Realtor extraordinaire who found this small home for me eight years ago and who has become a friend.

Without Liz sealing the deal I would not be sipping coffee outside, watching baby birds fledge while iris flowers bloom, butterflies arrive and fish rise to the surface in ponds, waiting to be fed. Thank you Liz. I am grateful every day to be here now.

It all started simply enough with a small dish of caviar placed at the edge of the swamp.

I sat back on my heels and waited. At nine years of age, sitting on my heels was easy. Having glimpsed a calico cat skulking in the swamp behind our quarters at Jacksonville Naval Air Station I wondered if a food lure would bring the cat closer to me.

And that caviar? Taken from the family kitchen without permission. Even at my young age I knew it was easier to get forgiveness than to get permission.

No cat showed up. The next day I returned and saw the dish was empty. Filling it again, I moved the dish a bit closer to our back door.

This routine went on for days. Never saw a cat. Finally, I opened the back door to our quarters, stuck a wedge in to keep it open and placed the dish on the kitchen floor. Then I sat cross-legged on the cool linoleum floor and waited.

The wait was not long. A female calico cat walked into the kitchen like she owned the place. Without looking at me she headed for the dish and ate the caviar. Then she came over an rubbed my hand.

That is how Ms. Purr Squeak came into our lives. She squeaked when she purred. My dad was so smitten with her that somehow an antique child's highchair appeared, sans tray, so Ms. Purr Squeak could join us for dinner every night.

Being a Navy family, we moved a lot. Ms. Purr Squeak, her age unknown, was part of the family and moved with us every time.

Years later when I was a senior in college and became engaged, my dad announced to my fiancée: "You marry my daughter you take the cat too."

And so, she lived with us. Inevitably the time came when she slowed down to a standstill. She passed away while I was expecting my second child. The vet estimated she was 20 years old. I miss her still.

Ms. Purr Squeak was the first of a long line of rescue cats. I found Eva a few years ago in the Sarasota County Humane Society outreach bus at a farmer's market. At six months old she grew up in the kitten room and was very social.

In her cage inside the bus, she was by herself, playing with a straw that had been tied in a knot – a makeshift toy. Even though she was alone, she was making fun happen. My kind of cat.

But after asking the adoption fee and hearing the cost was $80, I was ready to walk away. Then the volunteer remembered that the first three adoptions that day were free –

the Phillippi Farmers Market folks were paying. Serendipity. Eva came home with me.

She is a diva, the alpha cat. When Bella, my rescue dog, arrived last summer Eva walked right up to her, sniffed, and made it clear who was in charge. No problem. Bella, at 54 pounds, knew Eva, at 9 pounds was alpha.

Mango, at age one and a half, arrived a year after Eva. Same bus. Same Humane Society. Only this time people were crowded around cages of kittens while Mango, full grown, sat on the other side of the bus, totally ignored.

Mango was raised in the Humane Society kitten room, adopted at six months of age then returned a year later as the couple had a baby and said the child was allergic to cats.

Mango licked my hand. That did it. He came home with me. Do you see a pattern here? Once the fur ones make it through the front door of my home it is forever.

Took a while for Eva and Mango to work it out. He thought he should be in charge. Wrong. Now Mango is trying to work it out with Bella. He keeps acting startled that a dog is in the house. Get used to it. Fortunately, Bella is good with cats.

Last week I talked about baby birds in my back garden. I know what you are thinking – how can cats and birds exist in the same universe?

Simple. Create two universes.

There is only one house rule – no cats outside. Eva and Mango are inside cats, well fed, sometimes bored but never tiring of watching the world outside floor to ceiling windows – they see birds, bees, butterflies, squirrels – the works.

Is this cruel? Not at all. Safer for the cats and much safer for birds. People for the Ethical Treatment of Animals (PETA) have an article entitles "14 Billion Reasons to Keep Cats Inside." You can find it online. Cats kill wildlife over and over, not just the one mouse they bring home. Multiply that by the estimated 145 million cats and wildlife suffers severely.

Finally, if asked nicely, any cat will share the facts of life with you. Here they are:

Cats rule.

Dogs drool.

This is Cats, part two.

Ms. Purr Squeak came into our lives when I was in the second grade in Jacksonville. In grade eight my dad was stationed in Washington D. C. at the Pentagon.

Everywhere we move my dad built Ms. Purr Squeak an outside door to come and go (those were the days before we knew cats should be kept indoors). In D.C. her outside access was a ramp up to a kitchen window that my dad fitted with a flap opening.

Keep that image in mind.

One evening my parents threw a bash for diplomatic types. The living room and dining room were full of people.

I don't remember titles, but I do know a Russian (Ambassador?) arrived with two bodyguards who stayed on either side of him all evening. Both bodyguards wore oversize jackets. I assumed there was firepower underneath. I was an eighth grader but not totally naïve.

My mom set a gourmet buffet that included a huge plate of lobster pieces. The odor of fresh seafood touched the nostrils of Ms. Purr Squeak, a former swamp cat now allegedly domesticated.

Ms. Purr Squeak jumped up on the dining room table, glared at the assembly of people, emitted a loud, no-nonsense growl, and headed for the lobster plate.

The room went silent. Everyone stared at the cat. She grabbed a huge piece of lobster and backed across the table, still growling, still giving everyone a "bite me" glare.

The two bodyguards patted their jackets and moved closer to their Russian diplomat. All the guests stood frozen, drinks and plates in hand, and quite frankly, fascinated.

My mom was humiliated. She tried not to cry. My dad leaned forward. He wanted to see what the cat would do next.

Ms. Purr Squeak jumped down from the table, still holding the large lobster piece, backed towards her exit ramp, went up it backwards, turned around and disappeared through the flap, lobster and all, never to be seen again that evening.

All the guests started talking in exited voices. The story was retold different ways. What an evening! The two bodyguards stared hard at Ms. Purr Squeak when she made her exit. I may be imagining it, but I thought I detected a bit of admiration on their part for our cat's cheekiness.

Perhaps somewhere in a chateau there are retired diplomats sipping vodka and remembering the night a cat backed down a whole room full of people including a Russian diplomat with bodyguards.

Quite a story. The truth is I have found real life to weirder, wilder, and more wonderful than any fiction novel.

Which brings me finally to Grace, a rescue cat who passed away in 2017 at the age of 20. I wrote her eulogy. Here it is:

Grace died today.

She was 20 years old.

Grace and her four sisters were born in a horse barn in Ocala, Florida. When the owner saw the litter of kittens, he declared the kittens must be gone by that afternoon or drowned.

A barn worker started calling around and making the rounds. Grace arrived at my house smelling like a toxic waste dump. She had been dunked in flea dip; the same stuff used on horses. Dead fleas fell on the floor like pepper pieces out of a grinder.

Grace fit in the palm of my hand.

She did not belong here. There were already four cats and two dogs. But Grace had something about her. A look in her pale yellow/green eyes that spoke of ancient knowledge, perhaps directly delivered from Egyptian cats known for their farsightedness.

She was promptly named Grace. It suited her.

Grace was a reduced calico. That means her coloring was white with grey and pale gold spots instead of the typical calico white with black and gold areas.

The night Grace arrived we ordered pizza. No one can remember why. It wasn't something we did ever before.

The pizza arrived. We opened the box on the living room coffee table. Suddenly, a kitten streaked into the living room.

Grace leapt into the pizza box, eyes dilated, half crazed by the smell of cheese and tomatoes. She slid across the entire pizza, finally bumping up against the box.

I picked her up, dripping, as she licked cheese off her paws.

We never ordered pizza again.

On bright days Grace sunbathed on the screened in porch, sitting like a cat statue found in an ancient Egyptian tomb, her eyes evoking the one thousand yard stare.

I often wished I could see what she saw.

Grace took being born in a barn as a serious birthright. She was not shy about eating her food and anyone else's. Sleeping arrangements were hers to make and she snapped at any interruption.

Moving to Sarasota five years ago brought out surprisingly soft parts of her personality.

She discovered for the first time that I had a lap, and it was comfortable. In recent months, as she aged, Grace took over my lap, resisting any movement on my part to get up. This made morning coffee much longer than it used to be.

Graceful to the end, she passed quietly, her family nearby.

She is survived by her extended family – Tito, and Amy, rescue cats, and Obi, rescue Welsh Corgi, and her mom Lucy, whose lap is sadly empty.

Should you wish to honor Grace's memory, consider adopting an older cat from an animal shelter. Older cats, so full of warmth and asking so little in return, are passed by while people rush to coo at the kittens.

Or if you live at deed-restricted housing that does not allow animals, plant a tree to help Mother Earth or several milkweeds to help monarch butterflies.

After all, everything is connected.

Grace knew that.

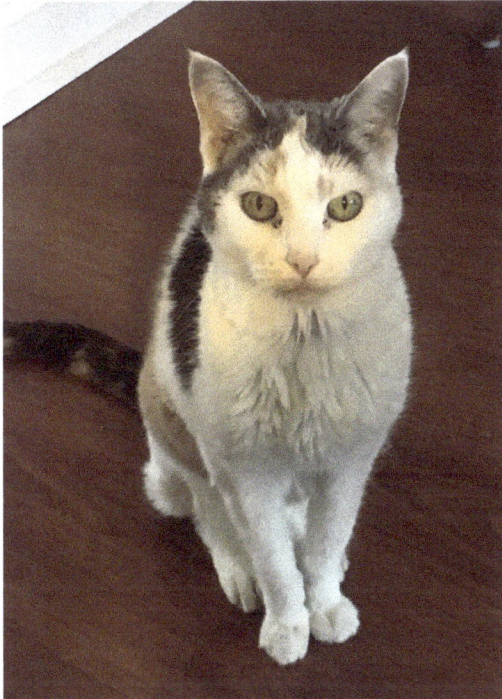

Evaporation. It happens every day in my outside ponds. How does evaporation work? Water from ponds, rivers, lakes, drainage ditches, etc., evaporated into the air, rising to get stuck in the clouds, then coming back down to earth as rain.

The cycle may be a bit more complicated than that. But you get the idea.

Right now, the cycle is broken. No rain. Clouds are hording water like people in the pandemic hording toilet paper and gasoline.

My pond levels keep getting lower and lower. Plus, I came outside one day last week and water in the bird baths (which I fill every day) had evaporated. That never happened before.

For the first time I am filling buckets with water from the hose. These sit for three days to let the chlorine evaporate naturally. Yes, hose water has chlorine and that must dissipate before putting the water into ponds. Chlorine kills fish.

And my four rain barrels? Empty. No rain.

On the bright side, literally, a new water lily in the middle pond is quite happy, putting out flowers with abandon – water lilies do their thing without ever realizing how breathtakingly beautiful they are.

Water lilies need at least four hours of continuous sunlight to bloom. They open from 10 a.m. to 2 p.m. then fold up again.

In the big pond purple water lilies announce themselves like trumpets playing a  fanfare. Ta dah! Behold beauty.

Back to the water issues – I worry for wildlife these days as they thirst for water during this drought. Installed more bird baths in both the front and back of my house. Also, some plates with water in them are placed on the ground – good for wildlife that slither and slide like lizards and snakes.

One dish is a puddling plate designed for butterflies. This is easy to do. Put sand, salt, and water in a shallow dish. Butterflies come, unfurl their proboscis and drink – they need the minerals and salt.

Are we having fun yet? I believe so. Meanwhile, no rain in the forecast.

This scenario reminds me of the science fiction book *Dune* by Frank Herbert. Water was so rare on Dune that if someone cried their tears were saved.

And American Indians had a dance just to encourage rain. As water levels continue to dip in the ponds from evaporation, I feel the need for a rain dance coming on.

Maybe a good time to dance is tonight with the total lunar eclipse and blood moon.

Just to hedge my bets, I'll keep filling buckets and praying for rain.

A ceramic vase on my veranda has a story to tell.

Wandering around a Goodwill store in Sarasota, Florida, for a first time visit, I spied a lovely hand painted vase made in Italy. Turning it over I see the price tag is $10.

Wow. I can do this. The vase would be a lovely addition to my veranda. I headed for the checkout desk and gently placed the vase on the counter.

The young clerk looked at the vase.

Then she looked up, inspected me, and said:

"Today is Tuesday."

I paused, clueless really, but thought it safe to agree.

"Yes, it is."

For the life of me I can't think what Tuesday has to do with anything.

The clerk gives me that pitying look, the one making it clear I did not read the memo.

"Seniors," she said, emphasizing the word, "get 50 percent off on Tuesdays."

Ah. Glorious! Sometimes it is great to be a senior. A hand painted vase for $5. Made my day. And now perhaps yours too.

When it comes to rain, it is still not happening. The forecast says rain. Skies darken. Thunder booms in the distance. But just a few drops fell into the dry bird bath. Within a few minutes those drops evaporate.

How bad is this lack of rain? Normally, the deep end of my big fishpond measures 17 inches. I measured it this morning. The depth is eight inches.

At this rate of evaporation, I will have to buy at least a thirty gallon aquarium, set it up inside the house, capture all the goldfish and move them inside so they survive.

In the meantime, Pastor Wes Bixby of First Congregational United Church of Christ in Sarasota could not resist a few riddles on Sunday morning during the 9 a.m. outdoor service.

Here are two:

What is the one question you can never say "yes" to?

How many months have 28 days?

As for the answers, stay tuned. All will be revealed in next week's Wednesday Notes.

To close, it feels great to be back on my bike after a two year absence. Had it tuned last year but never rode. There are always excuses. I took the computer off the bike and put it in a safe place. Translation: I never found it again.

Giving up the search I bought a new bike computer and Jeff at University Bike Garage along with his son Jordon installed it for me.

Time to ride. I rode six miles on Saturday on the Legacy Trail at a whopping average speed of seven miles per hour.

A gigantic gopher tortoise sat in the grass on the side of the trail and turned its head to watch me pass. I wanted to cheer. Such a good view!

While riding, people kept shouting out ON YOUR LEFT.

That is the protocol for passing on a bicycle. I was passed, passed, passed.

But hey, I am back on the road. Get ready. My day will come when I too say ON YOUR LEFT.

First things first. The answers to last week's riddles.

What is the one question you can never say "yes" to?

Answer: Are you asleep yet?

How many months have 28 days?

Answer: All of them.

And a bonus riddle for today:

What food needs to be broken before it can be eaten?

The answer is at the bottom of today's Wednesday Notes.

Rain has finally happened more than once. Outside, the pond levels are up. Plus, eggs appeared on the tops of lily pad leaves in the middle pond. These are frog's eggs. Exciting!

And I have discovered that a mystery fish lives in the big pond. It is black, and the liner is black, so no contrast like the orange goldfish.

I am doing the daily ritual of throwing tropical fish flakes into the pond. A large (eight inches long) black fish breaks the surface.

What a shock! Is this some panfish maybe deposited here as a fish egg by one of the many visiting birds?

Another shock – baby goldfish have been born.

Why is this a shock? If you are faint of heart, you might want to avert your eyes and move past the next paragraph. It is graphic.

Goldfish eat their young. Makes no sense but they do it anyway. Eggs hatch. Tiny fish emerge. The parents dine on their newborn children. Nauseating.

The young that survive do so by hiding in plant roots

Life has it patterns - beginnings, middles, and endings. Plus, patterns are everywhere. Look around. This photo is a pattern on the floor of the Bistro restaurant at the Sarasota Art Museum of Ringling College.

As promised here is the final riddle answer:

What food needs to be broken before it can be eaten?

Answer: An egg.

A hard rain raised pond levels a bit! Plus, rainwater fills the rain barrels. Life is good. I am grateful.

Meanwhile, there is a whole lot of sex going on in the big pond. The goldfish had babies, as you know. Yesterday while netting rubber tree leaves out of the pond, I happened to net a big trapdoor snail. Attached to its shell were five more snails of various sizes.

At this pace I will have change the pond rating from "suitable for all audiences" to "PG 13 parental discretion advised."

In the online art world Sketchbook Revival has couple of weeks every year where videos of artists doing a project are posted twice a day.

One artist, Jean Oliver, known for her large, commissioned paintings, told a story about hiking one day with her husband. They came across a senior citizen with a small sketchbook and small bag with all her painting needs.

"Oh, I want to be her one day, able to go out and paint!" Jean said.

"What is stopping you from doing it now?" her husband asked. Soon she developed a free course on packing light to go forth into the world and paint.

Jean advises keeping a sketchbook with you all the time, perhaps in a back pocket or purse, for those times when you wait in an office or are sitting at a restaurant waiting for a friend to arrive.

Instead of turning on the cell phone and looking at email and the latest Facebook feed, all of which will increase your stress levels, leave the phone off and reach for the sketchbook.

I've been giving this a go. It works. Sometimes I just doodle, other times look around at what might work in a small drawing.

Outlining leaves and creating a world inside the outline has intrigued me. My attempt is watercolor and pen and ink.

June is LGBT Pride month, so the leaves are a rainbow of colors and all of them are wonderful.

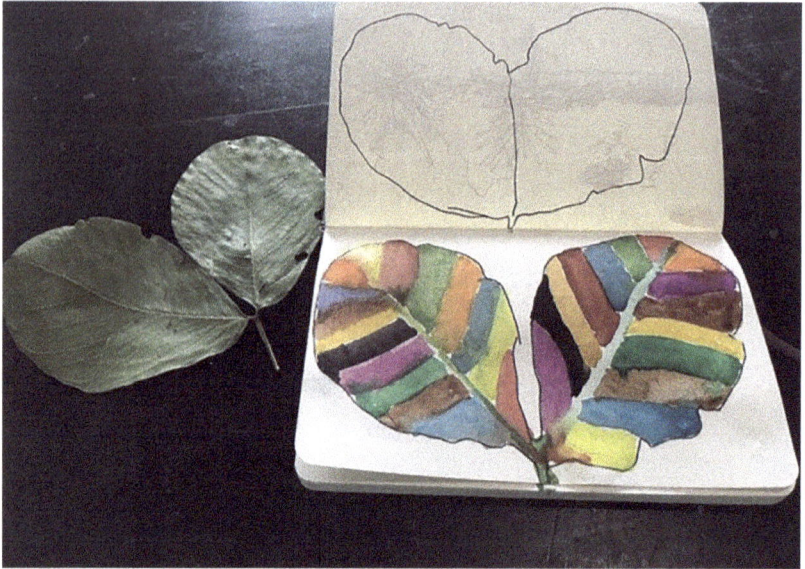

In life we are all different colors, sizes, gender, race, nationality, sexual orientation, abilities, age, you name it.

A racist thinks these differences means separate people and put them on different shelves by their value. An anti-racist knows we are all equal in our differences. We are all on the same shelf!

Equal in our differences. This concept is a big takeaway for me from Ibram Kendi's book *Be Anti-Racist*.

And all God's children said . . .Amen.

I wrote this column for Father's Day back in my newspaper days. My dad, Robert Park Beebe, has passed away since then but today, in honor of all dads, I'm sharing those thoughts again.

"It is 3660 miles to Tahiti," my dad says while pointing a finger out his living room window in Carmel, California. The sun is setting in the west. Tahiti is out there, calling him to sail away on the evening tide.

Robert Park Beebe – master mariner, retired Captain, United States Navy, naval architect, pilot, and my dad.

For years as a naval architect and in addition to his U.S. Navy profession, dad worked on graceful boat plans for other people. He also designed his own original dream boat and called it the Passagemaker – with both sail and motor round the world capacity.

After retiring from the U.S. Navy, Dad had the boat built in Taiwan, sailed the seven seas, and wrote a book about passagemakers.

A Vermonter by upbringing, dad stands 6'4" tall with the long legs that run in our family. He lives his life on 24 hour time. If dad says "be there at 0800" then set your watch and be there at 0800.

I recall cooling my heels outside a San Francisco hotel dining room. I am about eight years old and have been given one free hour on my own. It is also, I realize, a test in time telling,

Dad expects me to be in the dining room at 12 noon sharp. I arrive early, take a sea, and wait. As the second hand begins to sweep up towards noon, I make my entrance.

My family is seated in the dining room. Dad looks up at me, then at the clock on the wall that strikes the hour at that moment. I receive a slightly surprised nod of approval. For a Vermonter, known for being taciturn, that gesture from dad is high praise.

Somewhere in the layer of memories I recall a Valentine's card. It is elegant with hearts and flowers embossed on parchment. The signature reads:

FROM A SECRET ADMIRER

My mom would look at the card, oh and ah, and wonder who could the secret admirer be? I professed to be clueless, but I knew the answer and kept it secret.

Growing up I received a card from a secret admirer every year on Valentine's Day.

The signature was always done in a neat block handwriting that bore a striking resemblance to the engineering block alphabet that dad used to letter his boat plans.

And so, Happy Father's Day to dad

FROM A SECRET ADMIRER.

When the sun comes up, I step out of the house and onto the veranda, fish food can in hand. The goldfish, plus assorted mosquito fish and my mystery fish, all know I am coming.

This is our morning routine. They shimmer on the surface, trying their best to inveigle their way into me giving them a bigger pinch of fish flakes.

Inveigle. A word you do not see often. Every day I get the Merrian-Webster Word of the Day as an email. Inveigle, a verb, arrived on Monday. It means to persuade someone to do something by means of deception or flattery. Like hand out more fish flakes by shimmering on the surface of the pond.

Every email includes the word of the day, trending words and a word quiz. The current quiz is Name That Color. Some are obscure. Feeling competitive? Take the quiz then compare your score with different age groups.

Writers know one word leads to another. Pretty soon there is a sentence followed by a paragraph and, gasp, before long a chapter – a book in the making.

I see heads nodding. Before you ask, no, I am not currently working on another book. A topic would have to be very enthralling to get my attention these days. Hard to concentrate when the future is so uncertain.

But I love words and I am always excited by a blank page. Ah, possibilities both verbal and visual. While going through long neglected storage boxes looking for a column I once wrote about my dad for Father's Day (found it) I came across a dummy.

Not the stuffed kind. This is a picture book dummy made when I was dreaming a children's book. A dummy helps organize text and pictures, particularly for children's book.

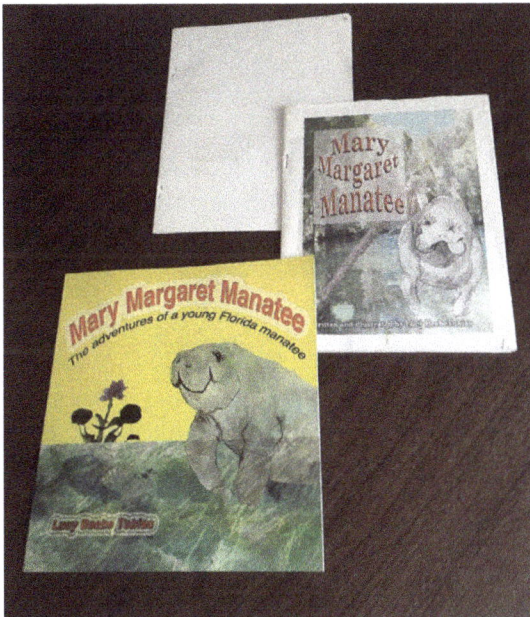

Made of plain paper to the right number of pages.

Mine is simple. Folded legal sized paper, stapled. I made an early dummy of my Mary Margaret Manatee story as it existed then. Took this dummy with me to a children's book illustration class taught by Jennifer Houdeshell, a marvelous children's book illustrator,

I read the dummy book out loud to the class. They were so supportive. Jennifer became a friend, cheerleader, mentor.

It took six years to see *Mary Margaret Manatee the adventures of a young Florida manatee* published, so the words "early stages" lasted a long time.

Here is this week's mission for you:

Stack four or five blank sheets of paper together. Fold the pile in half. Staple along edge if desired.

This is your book dummy. Put it next to your plate at mealtimes. Carry it around. Have it nearby for morning coffee. Inhale the blank pages. Dream. Visualize. Think of a title.

Then turn to page one a write the first word.

Have fun. Develop a story. Doodle some drawings.

You do have a book within you.

Yes, the ponds are full, almost overflowing! Rain. Lots of rain. Grateful.

All that rain happened while I was away for several days in St. Augustine, my first away time since lockdown last year.

While there I had a mission – light two candles at the Mother Mary statue inside the Cathedral Basilica of St. Augustine.

Tried the church door on Saturday but it was locked.

This candle ceremony started when my dad had a heart attack decades ago in California. I visited the Carmel Mission every day and lit candles. I thought if I could light enough candles he would live. Sadly, that was not so.

But the ritual remained in my DNA. When traveling, I'll find a catholic church (the only ones that have candles) and I light two candles. One for all those people I've loved and lost and one for all the living that I love. And I stay a while to name them all.

On a bike and barge trip a few years back, we had a choice one day of riding bikes in the rain or going off on our own (and presumably staying dry). I chose the latter and decided to look for a church. Five folks joined me.

We found an old catholic cathedral in sad shape. Rainwater oozed down walls. Benches had been removed. We wandered around, looking for candles. Found them at the Mother Mary statue area.

Right next to her tall statue was a small statue of St. Margaret. One of the women in our group was named Mary Margaret. We thought the same thing – that we were exactly where we needed to be.

All of us lit candles then sat quietly for a half hour or so. That memory lingers. I like to think those candles are burning still, lifting the people we love to eternal light.

Back to St. Augustine. On Sunday morning the cathedral doors opened for mass. In I go, heading straight for the Mother Mary statue area. I've been here before on the same mission. It felt like a homecoming.

My hand was shaking as I lit the first candle. The list of loss in my life grows longer. Last month my stepsister died. A few months before that my ex-husband and father of my sons died.

I lit two candles, one for the living, one for the dead. Then I sat for a while, calmed by the candle ceremony.

Not wanting to go back by the main aisle to exit the church, mass was about to start, I saw a door not far from the Mother Mary statue. A parishioner held mass bulletins and stood next to the door.

Is this an exit I asked her. Yes, it can be. She opened the door. I step into a small walled courtyard I've never seen before. There is a bronze statue of a missionary. I'm thinking – must be yet another Jesuit or Dominican being praised for bringing the natives to the faith when the truth is indigenous people were being subjugated and put into slavery, all in the name of God.

I know. Harsh thoughts. And I was wrong.

A sign said: Padre Felix Varela, Havana 11-20-1788. St. Augustine 2-25-1853

Beloved member of St. Augustine community. Main ideological founder of the Cuban nationality. Educator, philosopher, speaker, and writer. Advocate of human and civil rights in Cuba and U.S.A. Advocate of popular education and religious freedom. Pioneer of American Catholic journalism . . .

WOW! What a discovery – found by walking through a different door.

# Summer 2021

The color of the day is orange – and I found lots of orange in my life. A Gulf fritillary butterfly, a pagoda plant in full bloom, a ceramic fish with orange fins and tail, an orange umbrella, and firebush in bloom with red-orange flowers.

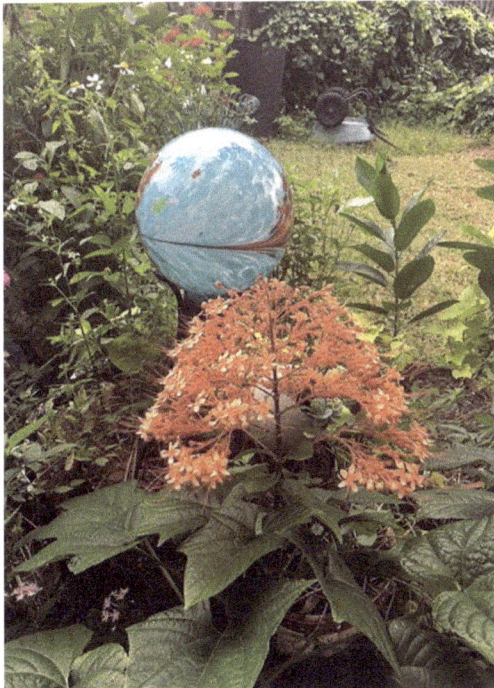

Jeff Nurge, a Florida native plant enthusiast in South Florida, advises anyone wanting to go native in their gardens to start with firebush that is attractive to birds, bees, and butterflies.

Jeff and his Native Choice Nursery are in the nursery chapter of my book *The Zen of Florida Gardening*. He has a newsletter with lots of native plant ideas for every season.

When I moved to Sarasota my realtor did not mention that Sarasota can be Windy City. High winds seemingly out of nowhere. On one blustery day the waterfall, standing tall over the middle pond, was knocked over by wind and landed on the ground below the pond.

Water followed gravity downward. By the time I ventured outside and saw what was happening, most of the pond water was gone, drained onto the ground. Fish were swimming with their fins showing above the remaining water.

Solution? A planter placed on top of the waterfall. Hopefully heavy enough to keep the waterfall in place when the winds blow. So far so good.

Even during a recent storm with a name – Hurricane Elsa. Turned out to be a nonevent, thank goodness. Lots of rain, some wind. Standing water remains on the path around the big pond and on the veranda.

The water level of the in the ground pond is up over the rocks. Goldfish, fortunately, are not the least bit interested in swimming over the rocks onto the veranda. Such an adventure would not end well for them.

A final flash of orange – my car is an orange Honda Fit. Had Hondas for a long time. While waiting to sign the papers the service guys, who knew my previous Honda well, came out to congratulate me.

One of them spotted an orange stainless steel water bottle on the table.

"You didn't buy this car to match your water bottle, did you?" he asked.

I smiled and said nothing. He walked away shaking his head. Ten years later I still have the orange car and the orange water bottle.

Where is the orange in your life?

Have you ever worn a friendship bracelet? My young granddaughter Finn and I giggled a lot as we tied friendship bracelets on each other's wrists. Then we went to the kitchen and made cookies. Ah, happy times.

One bracelet website says:

"Originally, these colorful bands were invented by native people in Central and South America. According to tradition, you tie a bracelet onto the wrist of a friend who may wish for something at that moment. The bracelet should be worn until it is totally worn-out and falls off by itself, at which moment the wish is supposed to come true."

For creative types who want to make friendship bracelets there are a lot of patterns with names like Chinese ladder, zig zag, chevrons. Often these bracelets are made with embroidery floss. Many designs are easy for children to do.

Not feeling crafty but ready for an old idea to come around again – I recently bought some friendship bracelets online.

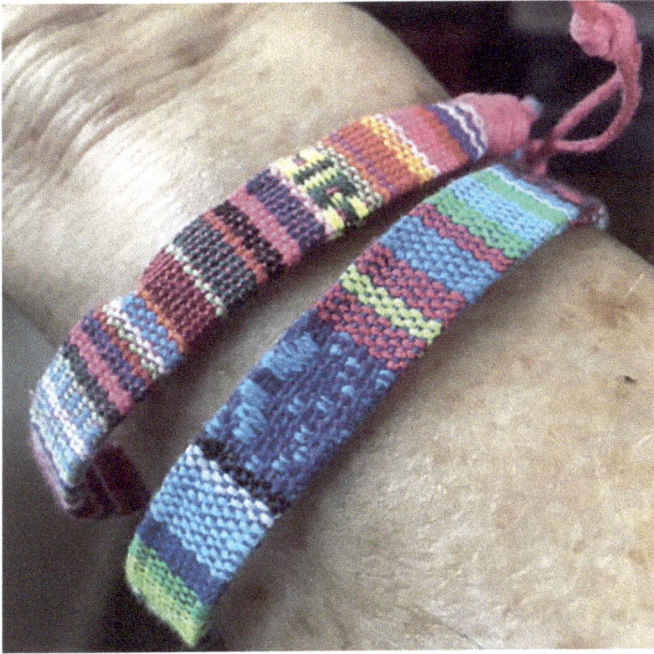

Wearing one in solidarity with a longtime friend who has elected for major surgery that will happen soon. The other one is reminding me of a commitment to exercise five times a week.

The bracelets stay on all the time – in the pool, the shower, around town. They are quick dry. I'm liking these visual ties that bind – connecting me to people and projects.

Meanwhile, being indoors during afternoon rains offers an opportunity to declutter closets and open storage boxes long ignored.

In one box I found a page (no attribution) on getting creative that suggested wearing different hats for stages of creativity:

When you are searching for new information, be an explorer (picture a pith helmet).

When you are turning your resources into new ideas, be an artist (picture a French beret).

When you are evaluating the merits of an idea, be a judge (picture the fake wigs judges wear).

When you are carrying your idea into action, be a warrior (picture a medieval armor helmet).

What will you be this week – explorer, artist, judge, or warrior? Choose your hat.

If you believe the earth is flat, then you should stop reading right now. I'm serious.

What comes next is about the earth being round, plus the earth rotating around the sun and what that all means for my back garden.

Therefore, if you believe in the scientific fact that the earth is round then continue reading.

Facts: The earth's rotation or earth's spin is the rotation of planet Earth around its own axis. It also has a rotation axis in space, making one revolution around the sun that takes about 365 days.

Where are we in that cycle? I do not know. But I do know the sun earlier this summer rose in the east and shed first light on the veranda. These days the sun casts its first rays along the fence line, abandoning the veranda.

My ponds, located next to the veranda are feeling the effects of more shade. I confess it took me a while to notice the change.

Water lilies need a good four hours of sun a day to bloom. The big pond still gets that at midday. Lilies are blooming. But the middle pond, already sheltered by the large overhanging rubber tree, has one white water lily and it is now dormant. The middle pond is completely shaded now that the sun has moved its position.

The third pond, completely under the rubber tree, is full of aquatic plants desperately reaching their leaves in any direction, twisting, turning hoping to catch some sun rays. They are not having success.

In among those leaves is a lotus soon to bloom. That is an awesome thought! Will it happen? Only the sun's position knows.

This is the one year anniversary of the death of Georgia Representative John Lewis. In 2020, he was asked by an interviewer what he would say to people who feel as though they have already been giving it their all, but nothing seems to change.

Lewis answered: "You must be able and prepared to give until you cannot give any more. We must use our time and our space on this little planet that we call Earth to make a lasting contribution, to leave it a little better than we found it, and now that need is greater than ever before."

And here is his excellent, radical advice to make some noise and get in good trouble.

"Do not get lost in a sea of despair," Lewis tweeted almost exactly a year before his death in 2020 of pancreatic cancer. "Do not become bitter or hostile. Be hopeful, be optimistic. Never, ever be afraid to make some noise and get in good trouble, necessary trouble. We will find a way to make a way out of no way."

Lewis had a long history of good trouble, including 24 arrests for civil rights events.

Making some noise and getting into good trouble. It can happen anytime. Like last weekend at a craft event when I shared a table with another book author. She was bitter about life including the fact her children's books were turned down by a local library because all the characters were white. She was urged to put some diversity in her stories by adding Black children. That set her off on a rant. Why should the world have both Black and white children?

I took a deep breath. Did I want to get involved? No. Is this an important issue? Yes.

A lightbulb went off.

"So," I suggested, "Look at the people walking by our table, tell me what you see."

White, Black, Asian, Hispanic, senior citizens, teenagers, couples with young children, persons of both sexes using canes, walkers, wheelchairs.

She saw it. Diversity. Flowing right past our table. This is real life. Perhaps her next book could have the main character making a new friend from a different culture. Just a thought.

Authors of books for children need look no further than Ezra Jack Keats (1916-1983) for inspiration. He is the Caldecott Medal-winning author of *The Snowy Day*.

This book broke new ground (made some noise) in 1962 as one of the first children's picture books to show a real life multicultural urban setting. I have this book and look at it often for inspiration.

So, no matter what path you walk in life, make some noise, and look for good trouble.

Find a way to make a way out of no way.

On Sunday morning a zebra longwing began laying eggs on blue passion vine leaves. She deposited an egg on one leaf, then another on a new leaf, with much fluttering in between.

This is a consuming job, laying eggs. So much to do, so little time. A butterfly's life span is about two weeks. The next generation must make it! More fluttering. More egg laying.

Sitting on the veranda, sipping coffee, I watched the zebra longwing make her way to yet another leaf. I wondered if she realized that she had found the only remaining stem of passion vine left in my garden. Everything else has been eaten down to the stem.

Did you know zebra longwings are the state butterfly of Florida? What kinds of hoops did zebra longwing enthusiasts have to jump to make this happen? Was it a unanimous vote? Were there other contenders? Did they storm the state capital in Tallahassee to get their way?

In 1996, the state legislature named zebra longwings as the official state butterfly. How this came to pass is a mystery to me and surely of no concern to the zebra longwing currently laying eggs in my back garden. But should you be asked the state butterfly question in a trivia quiz, you now know the answer.

While feeding goldfish in the big pond this morning I did a head count, or fin count, whichever is correct. There are the original four goldfish plus six more, current total is ten.

Please remind me not to buy more goldfish. They are populating the pond quite well on their own.

Inside, doing a labyrinth story for a magazine, I reflected on some of my favorites – including a meandering contemporary labyrinth in a private garden in Jacksonville. At the center of this labyrinth sits a statue of St. Francis.

I am a big fan of St. Francis. He got it right. Love one another. Everything else is background noise. My St. Francis statue, next to a bird bath, has hands cupped so it can also serve as a bird feeder. St. Francis and birds go well together. It is said he used to sit in the woods, preach out loud, and birds came to listen.

Thinking about labyrinths, I moved St. Francis over to the labyrinth I painted on the veranda. This is where he needed to be. I was just slow to realize the fact.

I put birdseed in his cupped hands. Within a few minutes five mourning doves were pecking at seeds on the ground while a blue jay sat on St. Francis' head and another blue jay stabbed at the sunflower seeds in his hands, sending more seeds to the ground.

Did I mention all this wildlife activity happened on a Sunday morning? And I haven't even gotten to the lizard who lost half its tail . . .a tale yet to be told.

Rain puddles on the veranda even as more rain falls, putting rain dimples on the surface of my ponds, making goldfish rise to check out the action.

Water levels are high in all three ponds. That is a good thing. Raindrops sit like wet jewels on pond leaves.

Bella, my rescue dog, like all my dogs before her, is convinced that rain somehow is under my control, and I could make the wet stuff go away. Not happening. She sits inside, morose pouting as she has no desire to go out and get wet.

Last week, on a sunny day, I assembled the shovel, handsaw, rake, pitchfork, clippers, broom, wheelbarrow, gardening gloves, roll of edger material, stakes, hammer, level, measuring tape, pavers, rocks, and edger spade,

Whew! When working on the new path it takes all those tools and materials along the way. I confess. I have been on a path making hiatus. A few weeks ago, while digging I ran into a rubber tree root that needed to be cut out by a handsaw. That just got to be one tree root too many. So, I took a breather. But now I am back.

Did I mention how not fun it is to cut tree roots out of the ground with a handsaw?

And I should mention what great fun it is to visit botanical gardens and be inspired. Like Bok Tower Gardens in Lake Wales, Florida

I want to share a quote by Edward Bok, a man of peace who had a way with landscaping and with words:

"Wherever your lives may be cast, make the world a bit better or more beautiful because you have lived in it."

Wednesday Notes, August 11, 2021

"She'll be coming around the mountain when she comes." Sing it with me now . . .and I'm thinking of changing the lyrics to "She'll be coming around the bend when she comes."

The new path being built in my back garden is coming around the bend finally. This oval path, some 60 feet in length, will take up the center area of my garden.

This path will wind past a plethora of plants – red penta, pink penta, spider plants, candlestick cassia, bamboo, pagoda plants, sweet potato vines, coontie cycads, vincas, shrimp plants, white Mexican penta, banana plant, Spanish needles, milkweed tree, Florida cranberry, Simpson's stopper, assorted succulents, a few zinnias in bloom, and volunteer plants that have yet to tell me their names.

Joining the plants in the center area – a ceramic fish, a solitary bee house, a bird bath, a toad abode, a gazing globe, and even a sign saying "butterfly garden" but the butterflies knew that already.

I appreciate this path project, tree roots and all. Working on it bit by bit has elevated my mood, given me an energy spike even now with the Delta variant depressing everyone and the dog days of summer forcing us all to stay inside and forget outdoors.

True, midday is hot and humid, but mornings and evenings are fair game for outside projects.

A new small round solar water fountain arrived. It is floating in the big pond. Came equipped with five different heads. Fun trying them out! Warmed by midday sun, water patterns push right up into the air! At $14.95 the solar water fountain is, as they say, a cheap thrill.

Meanwhile another tropical storm, this one named Fred, has Florida in its cone. Lucky us. Time to get the small glass top tables indoors, turn all the outside chairs on their sides, turn the large glass top table upside down (making it harder for wind to blow it away), bring in the umbrella – the usual bad weather prep.

Speaking of weather . . .in my job as Authentic Florida expert for Visit Florida a few years back, our crew of four (two camera people, project manager and me the standup) traveled around the state making videos.

One time we were in Pensacola, inside the Pensacola Museum of History (formerly T.T. Wentworth Jr. Florida State Museum), talking with the director about Pensacola history.

Native Americans were around long before the Spanish arrived by ship in 1559. Spanish conquistador Don Tristan de Luna came with a convoy of wooden ships loaded with everything needed to start a permanent colony – families, livestock, grain, soldiers.

Everyone went ashore, but then, in just a few weeks, along came a hurricane. All the ships were destroyed. Survivors spent the next three years waiting to be rescued. So much for starting a colony. And that is the short version of Pensacola events. (Note: all this happened six years before Pedro Menendez de Aviles founded St. Augustine in 1565)

We asked the director to stand in front of an exhibit of the ships and talk about that landing in 1559. Before the shoot I took him aside to offer some advice.

I said, "Please do not use the word hurricane."

He looked astonished. "You are kidding, right?"

"No, sir. Hurricanes drive visitors away from Florida. We are not allowed to use the H word."

"But it was a hurricane that destroyed the ships and most of their supplies."

"Trust me, if you use the H word, they will delete it."

The director took a deep breath.

Camera time. He stood in front of the display case, pointed to the diorama behind him and then, looking right at the camera, described a "severe weather event" that destroyed ships.

Good man. I stood off to the side, smiling.

Later the crew and I went upstairs to the second floor balcony of the museum. King Jan Carlos 1 and Queen Sofia of Spain stood on this balcony in 2009 waving to a crowd of some 6,000 people massed in the square below.

They came to celebrate Pensacola's 450th anniversary.

I got to stand on that balcony, look at the camera, and tell that story, and even wave to the crowds (well, imaginary).

Look closely at the beehive photograph. See the closed hole on the lower right hand side. This sealing the hole with mud or clay was done by a mason bee to seal its eggs inside.

Mason bees are solitary bees. They do not produce honey but are terrific pollinators, visiting huge numbers of flowers every day.

A female mason bee is busy collecting pollen that will be stuffed into a cavity (like the bamboo holes in a mason bee house). Up to ten eggs are laid on top of the pollen. Female eggs in the back, males up front.

The opening is sealed with mud or clay, hence the name mason bee. Males emerge first, break the seal, wait for females to come out, mate, and the process starts all over again.

Putting a mason bee house in your garden is a great way to help increase the presence of pollinators. Situate the house in the shade. Facing southwest is best. Off the ground or better yet, hanging from a tree limb or on a fence – to deter predators.

Do not fret. Mason bees are not aggressive and will not bite unless, say, you decide to pinch one. And why would you do that?

Bottom line: mason bees are not interested in you. Funny isn't it, that not everything in life is about us.

Mason bees are way too busy getting on with their short (two weeks or so) but extremely productive lives. Help them out. Mother Nature thanks you in advance.

Meanwhile, as the mason bees do their thing, the new path under construction finally rounded the top curve of the path's oval shape. Toot! Toot! Pavers laid, edging pounded in, river rock added. Life is good.

Paver projects, ponds, and plenty of plants – this is what happens when you live in the same place for ten years, join a butterfly club, give, and receive pass-along plants, take classes, go to plant sales and make too many visits to garden centers.

Plus, I write books about gardening. The most recent is *The Zen of Florida Gardening*, Sea Aster Press, October 2020, all about unexpected moments of beauty and personal transformation that happens when you dig in the dirt.

Today – look for flowers blooming.

Today – find ways to pay it forward.

Today – seek out people who make you laugh. Spend time with them.

Buddha has an acute case of summer scum. His normal neutral grey color is obscured by a dark green coat of mildew deposited by daily summer rain.

Fear not, help is near. Buddha is about to get a rehabilitating spa day that included a serious bleach bath followed by a rinse and drying out in the sun.

Purchasing outdoor bleach brings up the subject of voting with our wallets. We do. And it matters.

The kind of products we buy, the packaging, the places we chose to spend our money – these are economic, environmental, and political decisions with consequences.

Buddha of course stays serene. And glad to be clean.

Should you need some serenity, I recommend walking the labyrinth at Unity of Venice, at 125 N. Jackson Road, Venice, Florida.

Think about it. Walking a labyrinth is perfect pandemic pastime. No social distancing required. Most likely you will be the only person at the labyrinth. No masks required. The labyrinth is outdoors.

Many phrases describe a labyrinth and its possible wellness effects. One phrase that stands out for me – radical equality.

A labyrinth does not care if your feet are large or small, perfect, or deformed, painted toes or no painted toes, brown feet or white feet, young tootsies or old tired feet, shoes, or no shoes.

A labyrinth welcomes you when you arrive with a heavy heart or if you skip and sing around every curve. If walking isn't working for you then sit near the labyrinth and trace a finger labyrinth.

Whoever you are and wherever you are on life's path, you are welcome to walk a labyrinth at your own pace and in your own way.

A labyrinth is not a maze. There is one path in and the same path out. You cannot get lost.

I like to walk this labyrinth very slowly, taking in the outline of plants and garden statues, thinking about the steppingstones in our lives.

The keeper of this garden labyrinth at Unity is Mary Badeau. She is constantly changing up the plantings on the path. Recently we connected as she was taking out blue pots and replacing them with white pots containing succulents.

I am thankful for labyrinth caretakers like Mary Badeau. She is a blessing.

She looked at me with her beautiful honey colored eyes. And her eyes asked this question:

Are you a good person?

My response: I try to be.

That was our moment. We bonded on the spot. It was all over but the paperwork.

She was not the dog I was looking for, but she is the dog I need. As my friend Rick noted "She was looking for you long before you found her."

Bella (my name for her) is a mixed breed rescue from Citrus County Humane Society. She came into my life on July 11, 2020.

Abandoned in a park, the shelter manager thinks she was taken for a car ride (she loves car rides) then thrown out of the car along with another dog, smaller, perhaps a sister or daughter. She had obviously had puppies in the past. She came without references, resumes or date of birth or a name.

I named her Bella which means beautiful. Estimated to be five to six years old, she is housebroken and good with cats.

I hope she had a good life until abandoned but who knows what happened? A job lost in COVID19 times, a move to a place that doesn't take dogs, no money to pay to have her spayed – none of those make any sense to me for abandoning a dog.

If a cat or dog makes it through the front door of my home, they stay forever. I will say it is a good thing she gets along with cats. I have two indoor cats. One of them, Eva, is totally alpha meaning she is in charge so you can go find some other chair to sit on because she is staying right where she is.

Bella gets that. She weighs 60 pounds. Eva weighs 7 pounds. It is all about attitude.

When I introduced Bella to my back garden, I told her she had found the mother lode – a fully fenced yard with wild stuff growing some three feet deep from the fence, plus open areas that even get mowed occasionally. Plenty of room to run, roam, and crash through the underbrush for fun.

Bella arrived just in time. I had finished digging my third pond and was looking at digging up another area to make a water garden. That means even more open area would be consumed.

A few more projects like that and there would be no room to run in the back garden. Now Bella still has some grassy areas to chase toys, bite at the water coming from the hose, just be a dog. It is a good thing.

She loves biting water. Turn on the hose, spray it around and Bella chases the water, biting the flow. Fun! Makes me laugh. She gets thoroughly wet and shakes water all over the place. It takes a dog to remind me that having fun is fundamental!

True confession time: I do not do well living along. With kids grown and significant others gone. I have come to realize, especially in these pandemic times, that having a dog is vital to my health.

Every day Bella saves me from myself. She gives me a reason to get up in the morning – first to go outside, then breakfast. This routine happens seven days a week. It is not negotiable.

Bella is family. Pencil in the expenses and time. Worth every dime, every minute. Is there a dog in your life?

Every morning my dog Bella and I step out onto the veranda and perambulate the perimeter of our property. And every morning there are surprises.

Like seeing a cluster of fat swallowtail caterpillars on a pipe vine leaf. How wonderful! Future polydamas butterflies!

Last year wasps were stinging these caterpillars and killing them.

All is well with the world when caterpillars peacefully go through their metamorphic journey and emerge into a new life.

Speaking of journeys that have pivot points and are transformative, here is mine as a writer/photographer.

Long ago and not so far away there was a breakfast café in Homes Beach, Florida. The owner was a former waitress who worked for years to make her dream of her own restaurant come true.

Inside, towards the back, was a large, round table capable of seating up to six people. By unspoken rules this table was reserved for locals. Not only that but our bill was 10 percent lower at this table. Why? Because the former waitress was grateful for faithful customers – those of us who showed up all year long, not just during tourist season.

And so it came to pass that one Sunday morning I am sitting at the round table with other locals. We are catching up on gossip – who caught what while fishing and where? Who got nailed by the school crossing guard for speeding in the school zone? The guard's nickname was Dragon Lady. She was fierce, breathing fire and blowing a loud whistle on motorists who dared to speed in the school zone.

As the gossip spun on, the photographer from the local newspaper, The Islander, waked into the restaurant. He knew exactly where I would be sitting on a Sunday morning.

Walking up to the table he said "Lucy, get your portfolio together. You have an appointment to meet my editor this afternoon. I'm leaving for another job – my job is yours – go get it."

What? I was freelancing stories and photos for magazines. This newspaper opening was news to me. And so it came to pass that I interviewed for the chief photographer's job.

The editor liked my portfolio but found me short on newspaper credentials (nothing published in a paper). He gave me some tryout things – including a full page assignment.

Write about anything. Take photos. Develop film. Lay out page. Did I mention anyone who works at a small newspaper must wear many hats?

Luckily for me I had taken a darkroom course at the local community college and quite fallen in love with black and white photography and paying with light.

Plus, I knew just what subject to pick – what happened to old Ed? I heard that question often. And I knew the answer.

Old Ed for years had a houseboat tied up at the city marina. He sold bait 24/7. Ed sported a long scruffy beard and a cap permanently welded to his head. A small dog named Andre, possibly a Pomeranian, was carried in one hand and a brown paper bag covering a bottle with undetermined alcoholic contents stayed firmly fixed in the other hand.

Then old Ed disappeared from the city marina. What happened? I knew the answer. His houseboat was now tied up around the corner in a private marina, the same marina where I berthed my old Chris Craft cruiser.

Retired from selling bait, old Ed still had the same dog who badly needed a bath and the same rumpled brown paper bag.

I wrote the story of old Ed, took photos, developed the film in the newspaper's darkroom, laid out the full page. It ran and got lots of reader response. And the job was mine.

At that time the paper was owned by the New York Times, part of its regional group of newspapers. The Islander was later sold when the NYT bought the Sarasota Herald Tribune.

Being chief photographer meant taking photos developing black and white film and making prints for a staff of

13 full and part time people, all cranky and behind deadline. Also, I did a full page feature every week that I called IN FOCUS. It had a photo of me at the top holding a camera and looking very happy.

Indeed. I recall one morning standing knee deep in mangroves photographing mangrove roots while a blue crab snapped its claws at me, ready to take on the invader.

I thought, it does not get any better than this. Of course, the job paid practically nothing. Welcome to the bottom rung of the newspaper world. But every week was different and challenging.

Thus began a 26-year career that spanned different newspapers and job titles, all with the NYT group of regional papers.

It all started with breakfast at the café. Before the pandemic, I went back to that café for the first time in years.

The round table is still there. The original owner long gone. Now tourists sat at that table. The locals were all sitting at the counter. I joined them.

Talk centered around local gossip. Two big potholes on the main drag yet to be fixed (so lots of people to blame) and a waterspout that morning had everyone's attention.

A guy named Fred pulled out his cell phone to show photos of the spout. He passed the phone down the row of folks sitting at the counter. It was a big one all right. We were impressed.

"Fred," the waitress said, pointing up to the TV on the wall. "Isn't that your waterspout? Someone beat you to it getting it on TV."

Sure enough, same spout, with the local weatherman intoning a dire script. Fred moaned. We all shook our heads.

"Ah, Fred, next time," said the waitress, giving him a generous smile and topping off all our coffee cups.

I believe we all need to be soothed by nature's beauty, especially now when our past feels faded like an old photograph and our futures are riddled with question marks.

My photograph shows candlestick cassia blooming along my back garden fence. Easy to see how it got the name candlestick, with bright yellow flowers standing up tall like candle tapers.

Cassia is a host plant for sulphur butterflies. Their caterpillars are the same shade of green as the cassia leaves.

This awesome tall plant started out as a small cutting, a gift from Catherine LaBrie years ago when I volunteered at the garden maintained by the Sarasota Butterfly Club on the grounds of the Sarasota Garden Club.

Pass-along plants are the best. They come complete with stories and good memories.

Tall. Showy. Elegant. All words to describe a pagoda flower. One is blooming in my back garden. It is a butterfly nectar plant. Thank you to Char for passing along young pagodas.

Google says this about pagoda flowers:

The Pagoda flower, also known as Clerodendrum paniculatum, is an erect, open semi-woody shrub with large evergreen leaves and huge clusters of orange-red or scarlet flowers. Butterflies, especially swallowtails, love this plant. It is a bush with multiple stems and grows between three and five feet, spreading two to three feet across.

And finally, a photograph of Eva napping. Not a nature photograph! But you know you needed to see Eva today.

With tangy salt air and light drizzling rain as my companions, I circled the center of a labyrinth at Key West Garden Club at West Martillo Tower.

And I wondered – why don't I walk labyrinths in the rain and salt air more often? Plus, the location is amazing.

Fort Martello was one of three Civil War era forts built as a defensive chain around Key West. No cannons were ever fired. No soldiers died in battle at this fort. West Martello Tower is a National Historic Site.

Munroe County and the Key West Garden Club have a lend lease agreement in place since 1949.

Located at 1100 Atlantic Avenue on Higgs Beach, the Gardens are open every day from 9:30 a.m. to 5 p.m. Admission is free. Donations appreciated. Some nearby parking is free.

Set high on a hill overlooking the Atlantic Ocean this five-circuit labyrinth and a peace garden were added in 2020.

The labyrinth is surrounded by plantings of firebush and Mexican penta. There are benches.

All the garden areas are partnered with the old ruins, and it makes a lovely juxtaposition – especially placing a peace garden and labyrinth in a fort designed for repelling invaders

Whatever the club's board of directors decides to do, that is what happens. As a result, the gardens are continually evolving.

The club has an obvious love affair with orchids. Brick paths wander past a fountain, a waterfall, a fragrance garden, a butterfly garden, tropical plants, and a gazebo popular as a wedding destination.

A vaulted ceiling leads to a secret garden. Small, compact, this is an intriguing place, a blend of history and creative garden vision.

I walked all the paths twice. I would go back in a heartbeat.

Moving on, Key West is a city most fowl. After leaving the gardens at one point I had to stop so a rooster could amble across a street, and he was not even in the pedestrian right of way.

Fowls rule.

Then, walking along a sidewalk, a mother hen nudged her chicks out of my way, clucking at them, probably saying - humans are not to be trusted, give them plenty of room.

My plan after visiting the gardens – hang out with the blue morpho butterflies and much more at the Key West Butterfly and Nature Conservatory.

Located at 1316 Duval Street, conservatory hours are 9 a.m. to 4:30 p.m. General admission $15, seniors (65 and up) $12. Masks were required inside the conservatory.

Take off your wristwatch. You will want to stay here and forget all those other plans,

So many butterflies and little songbirds. I sat on a bench and watched a male songbird (name unknown) pick up several small twigs. Then he flew to a nearby bush and handed them to a smaller bird – his mate. She twined the offerings to fit with other branches. Nest building!

In the center, two flamingos inhabit a pond. Their names are Rhett and Scarlett. Rhett was making quite a racket.

A sign read: "Why is Rhett making so much noise? It is mating season and he is trying to get Scarlett to notice him."

That may explain why Rhett was stamping his feet on rocks as he vocalized. Scarlett ignored him.

Meanwhile butterflies flutter everywhere. If you want an over the top breathtaking butterfly experience with memories that will stay vivid and fresh – this is the place.

It was hard to move on, but I did.

I'm addicted to caffeine. And I can find a good local coffee shop quickly. One the way to Key West, I scored bigtime finding Baby's Coffee, billing themselves as the southernmost coffee roasters in America.

The address is 3180 U.S. Highway 1 MM15. Open Monday through Sunday from 6:30 a.m. to 4 p.m. Baby's Coffee occupies an unpretentious building where they roast awesome coffee and make open face bagel sandwiches along with key lime pie and pizza. Their parking lot is usually full.

My regret – not buying a bag of their fresh roasted coffee beans like Death by Coffee or Breakfast Roast. Can you say online shopping?

Mina Edison had a brilliant husband who was a workaholic. Edison would forget to show up for meals. He worked late inventing things and was known to fall asleep on a cot in his workshop.

In the afternoons he would fish on a long pier in front of their Fort Myers winter home. But there was no bait on his hook, Edison just wanted thinking time alone.

The Edisons built their home in 1886. Mina used her ingenuity to get things done – like build a swimming pool, something she wanted badly. I imagine the pool conversation went something like this:

"Edison dear, wouldn't it be lovely to have a swimming pool?"

Mummmmmmmmmm.

"Swimming would be good exercise for all of us."

Mummmmmmmmmmm.

"Would you like to take a walk with me to see a site I think would work?"

Mummmmmmmmmmmm.

"Think about this, building a swimming pool could be a test."

Hummmmmmmmmm?

"A test of your new invention, Edison Portland Cement."

Well . . .

"What are the stress loads needed? What thickness works? Building a pool could turn into a research paper for a journal."

Good idea.

Mina got her pool. Later she got a bonus – a concrete cistern. Way to go Mina!

The Edison and Ford Estates website has this to say:

"Built in 1910, the 50' x 20' swimming pool is believed to have been constructed using Edison Portland Cement and was one of the first residential pools. In a 1928 remodel, the Pool House with changing rooms and a shower and Tea House were added. Edison had a concrete cistern built in 1919 to provide large amounts of potable water for domestic use. The new cistern was designed to store rainwater captured from the roof tops of Seminole Lodge."

I like Mina a lot. In addition to getting creative at getting things done she loved to garden. It comes as no surprise to learn

there is a Mina Edison statue sitting on a bench in the Heritage
Garden. Dedicated in 2009, the sculptor is Don Wilkins.

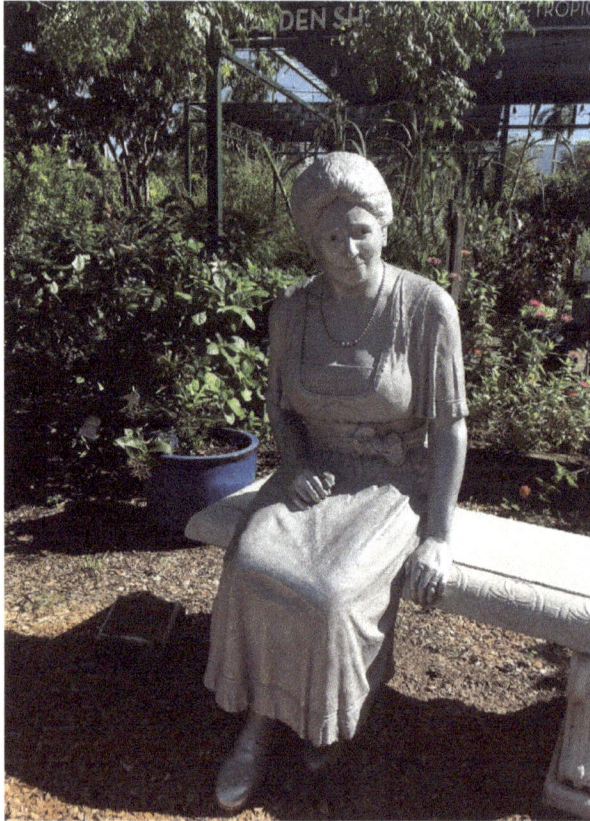

This is also the spot for the Edison Ford Garden Shoppe. There is an actual shop to go inside and a Garden Center outside with a tantalizing assortment of plants and trees, many of them native.

No charge to visit this area, it is separate from the Edison and Ford Winter Estates grounds tour. Many gardeners find their way here. We are like bees gravitating to pollen. This plant nursery is a must go to place.

On a recent trip down to the Florida Keys I took a slight detour to Fort Myers to visit the Garden Center. Found a variegated milkweed, a plant I had never seen before.

Bought it. Carried the plant down to the Keys and back home again a few days later. Milkweed is a host plant for monarch butterflies along with queen and soldier butterflies.

Upon bringing the plant home I discovered the smallest caterpillar I've ever seen on one the leaves. In just a week it has doubled in size.

Now the variegated milkweed sits in a big pot on my veranda next to a pond. This morning while writing this blog I looked out the French doors and saw a monarch caterpillar laying eggs on the milkweed. Oh my.

# FALL

Wednesday Notes, October 6, 2021

Some days, trying to see the big picture can be overwhelming – too many moving parts and conflicting facts. Why not take a break?

Stop. Stand still. Look at one thing closely. Good idea. Today is hereby declared to be UP CLOSE AND PERSONAL DAY. Go for it.

Got a magnifying glass? Take it outside. Look closely at bees extracting pollen on flowers, the tiny blossoms sprouting up in the grass, the thin cracks in the sidewalk.

One morning sitting outside and enjoying a slightly cool breeze that telegraphs the message – fall is on the way – I picked up the water glass, set in down in a different place and there, for a few seconds, sat a condensation ring, making its own artwork.

When I hear the words Florida Power & Light Company, I think, okay, their job is keeping the lights on. Indeed. But there is more. Much more as it turns out.

Consider Manatee Lagoon, an FPL Eco-Discovery Center® at 6000 North Flagler Drive in West Palm Beach. I didn't even know Manatee Lagoon existed until a friend told me.

This week I went to check it out and I am glad I did. Manatee Lagoon is adjacent to Lake Worth Lagoon, part of the Intracoastal Waterway.

Manatee Lagoon is open weekdays from 9 a.m. to 4 p.m. Closed on weekends. Both parking and admission are free. At the time of my visit, masks were required to use the restrooms. No masks needed for walking around the grounds.

I rolled into the parking lot at the same time two families were getting out of their cars. Must have been regulars – they headed straight for the walkway along the Lagoon with the children leading the way.

This is a prime manatee viewing area. I followed their lead. A large boat cruised along the Lagoon while a cool sea breeze carried the scent of salt water, sea creatures and a bit of mystery ingredients.

The breeze put a skip in my steps. So good to be out in fall weather and near the ocean!

Turn the corner at the end of the walkway and here is the discharge area for the huge Rivera Beach Next Generation Clean Energy Center. The power generated here goes to a grid that serves all of Florida.

What do manatees and generating energy have in common? Glad you asked.

When ocean water temperatures get cold in the fall and winter, manatees go looking for warmer water. Producing energy involves heating water to make steam that spins huge turbines and, voila, energy is made.

Steam is cooled using water from the lagoon. That water is returned to the lagoon, all nice and warm. Manatees find that comforting and congregate.

Obviously, the best manatee viewing times are say, late December or early January – cooler weather. But there is a great deal to be said for hanging out here anytime.

On the day I visited we all stood looking over the railing. A school of barracuda meandered around near the water discharge in the lagoon area. Bait fish by the hundreds darted back and forth.

Standing around reaped rewards! You guessed it. A manatee showed up. Cheers erupted. Video happened. Cameras clicked. Oh my. Quite thrilling.

At the present time a two-story building next to the lagoon is not open. Inside are interactive activities and a learning center about conservation and manatees. Check ahead of your visit to see if it is open or closed.

Adjacent to the parking lot are solar trees. If you click on a QR code with your cell phone, up comes a 3D animated junior solar tree called, appropriately enough, Sunny.

I did not do that. Instead, I returned to my car still smiling from seeing the manatee.

Did I mention Manatee Lagoon is free?

There is a time to hold 'em and a time to fold 'em. Good advice for both the game of poker and the game of life.

And it also works for garden projects. Like my first pond, installed after I had lived here for a year and saw how light and shadow played out over the seasons,

Put in a 40-gallon preformed pond at the end of the veranda under the huge rubber tree. Lots of shade.

Dressed it out around the edges with several tiers of wall pavers and plantings. The first crop of goldfish in the pond fell prey to a great white heron.

I went into battlefield mode, putting an outdoor chair in the pond so the heron could not get in and walk around. It worked.

Then found an outdoor plant holder, tall, and put that in the pond (it is a little hard to explain a chair in a pond).

Years went by peacefully. A lotus bloomed. The fish died out, but a frog took up residence.

Over the years two more ponds were installed, each one getting bigger. A second preformed pond at 120 gallons then digging a pond in the ground as a pandemic project ( I know, totally nuts).

The heron, or a relative, raided these ponds too. I put in hiding huts, bought new fish. Life went on in its unpredictable way.

Until recent months. The ecosystem in the small pond became unbalanced. Night marauders (raccoons) arrived and trampled down the plants, breaking all the stems. They also killed the frog.

The water became opaque, plants died, and the pond smelled like old bilgewater.

Time to fold 'em.

I emptied out the 40 gallon preformed pond bucket by bucket. To my surprise, at the last bucket an orange flash showed up in the water – one goldfish. How did it survive a heron, raccoons dying plants and stinking water all this time?

Survive it did. Now moved to the 120-gallon preformed pond to join four other goldfish.

Removed the 40 gallon tank from the veranda, exposing rubber tree roots that managed to grow under the pond.

I know my night marauders are raccoons because this morning I let my dog Bella out at 5 a.m. and she chased two big raccoons across the yard. I heard them scrambling up the six foot tall fence.

What to do? Looking at the Pond Guy website I found a sonic alarm to scare away midnight marauders. Ordered one.

Stay tuned. Who will win? Sonic sound or raccoons?

On a crisp fall day people from all walks of life gathered around a labyrinth at Rollins College in Winter Park, Florida.

The date: Thursday, October 21, 2021. The occasion: Dedication and blessing of a brand new 7-circuit labyrinth on the college campus.

While leaves fell quietly from nearby trees and a squirrel chattered, Rev. Katrin Jenkins, Dean of Religious Life at Rollins College began the litany of blessing.

We come today to bless and consecrate this reflective space.

Lifting our programs, we read the response:

As we circle around this ancient path, we welcome and embrace its power to heal and transform all who will come to walk its path alone or in community with others.

The journey to this awesome day started three years ago as both a dream and a calling to enact global peace and healing right here at this college campus.

At a labyrinth event in 2018, Jenkins, along with Frank Faine, Project Manager, Rollins Labyrinth Project, carefully unrolled a classical 11-circuit canvas labyrinth on the college green.

I joined them. Once the labyrinth was set up, we sat nearby, feeling like anxious fishermen casting a lure into a stream and hoping fish rise to the surface to check it out.

Students walked by, carefully avoiding direct eye contact. Still, they managed to look sideways at the labyrinth lying on the ground.

Some stopped. Jenkins or Raine got up, explained the walk, gave them a brochure. Several took off their shoes and walked the walk.

And so, a journey began that moved from portable labyrinth walks down a long and winding road traveled by Jenkins and Faine and others to this permanent sacred space and its possibilities – a journey filled with college meetings, education, countless prayers, and the process of gathering partners like the Legacy Labyrinth Project.

Labyrinths are found all over the world. But for the first time, at this dedication, I realized the word 'universal' has layers of meaning I never dreamed existed.

The Rollins College labyrinth is a Legacy Labyrinth. It joins six other Legacy Labyrinths all over the world. Each labyrinth is created to facilitate positive energy and compassion that spans the globe and connects them.

On dedication day we literally joined the other Legacy Labyrinths. Christine Katzenmeyer, executive director of the Legacy Labyrinth Project and Tisha Strauch, LLP program coordinator, came from Denver, Colorado for this dedication.

They brought with them small vials containing earth, sand other small pieces from all the Legacy Labyrinths. Each person standing around the Rollins labyrinth was given a vial. We opened our vials and, one by one added all those elements to a bowl passed around that contained small pieces from the Rollins labyrinth.

That mixture was placed into the earth around the college labyrinth. Now all the Legacy Labyrinths are literally connected. Wow!

Every time someone steps onto this Rollins College labyrinth they are connecting, supporting, and facilitating healing and inclusion for individuals and communities on a global scale.

Yes indeed. The word 'universal' has moved to whole new levels for me.

Also in the dedication service, two students, Lexi Shroll and Samantha Alenius, wrote and sang an original song called Seven Rings to celebrate the seven circuits of this labyrinth.

I listened to them sing and felt my heart lifting at the thought two students were transformed by the labyrinth experience and led to create music. As the guitar played and the harmonies unfolded, I felt assured the future is in good hands.

When photographers take a break, they sit around and talk shop. The subject often turns to light – artificial light, strobes, reflected light, natural light. We have an endless debate about light.

What is the best natural light for outdoor photographs – morning light or afternoon light? They are different.

Early morning light, my favorite, is soft and rather on the warm side, almost impressionistic, very little shadows to give anything volume. Things appear flattened, two-dimensional.

A morning glow will light up flowers, grass, trees, you name it – a light butter yellow color with a dash of pale coral. Some photographers prefer filters to sharpen up (or dampen down) the contrast. I am not one of them.

In the midday, sun overhead casts no shadows. Good time for any micro photography.

Afternoon light favors the cool side of colors. Lots of blues, reflecting sky. Objects have sharp dimensions and cast long shadows.

Definition matters in the afternoon. This is a good time to photograph tall buildings, houses, children at play. As a rule, afternoon photographs reproduce better in newspapers (where they will be rendered in black and white so high contrast is important).

These discussions about light, debates if you will, carried more weight back in film cannister days, especially when shooting Kodachrome or Ektachrome.

Now with the switch to digital cameras and all the dials to turn, it hardly matters what time of day it is.

Just for the record, most of my shooter friends prefer afternoon light.

Not me. I love the soft ambiance of morning light. Even now in the digital age. Maybe it has to do with being an early riser. Maybe all of this is subjective.

Sunrise. Morning coffee. Morning pages. Mourning doves cooing. Goldfish swirling at the surface anxious for breakfast flakes. Day lilies and pond poppies unfurling as they are warmed by the sun.

Breakfast. Daybreak. New beginning. All is forgiven. A new day. Embrace the possibilities of morning light.

Where do people go for a walk around water? In Tallahassee the answer is Lake Ella conveniently located one mile north of the Capitol. A wide sidewalk goes all the way around the lake for a delightful seven-tenths of a mile stroll.

I took that stroll this week. But first, a stop at Black Dog Café, a gourmet coffee shop. Black Dog on Lake Ella remains a Tallahassee fixture after 20 years, long enough that they recently decided it was time to put a whole new deck outside – a lovely place to sit with a view of the lake.

Some fifteen years ago I discovered Black Dog and Lake Ella while researching the Tallahassee area for my book *50 Great Walks in Florida,* published by University Press of Florida.

Black Dog was much more into counterculture then. Stepping inside for the first time I saw posters protesting many cultural and environmental outrages plus a lot of bumper stickers including one that read:

FRIENDS DON'T LET FRIENDS GO TO STARBUCKS

Right then and there, reading those words, I knew I'd found my place.

These days Black Dog looks more upscale. Photos and paintings by local artists adorn walls painted in muted colors. A small play area for children includes blocks, books, and a two-story dollhouse complete with furnishings.

They still specialize in local and single origin coffees plus baked goods. Their pecan bars need to be listed as one of the seven deadly diet sins. They sell out fast, which just shows you that sin is still in.

Fortified with a latte, I set foot on the sidewalk. Dedicated daily visitors bring food for the ducks. These birds are trained to spot softies. The ducks waddle quickly towards anyone with a bag in their hands. One woman was ahead of me the entire way around the lake, and bag in hand, she stopped to feed every gathering of ducks.

All around the lake are benches affording a good view of the large fountain that spurts up a tall column of water in the middle of the lake. There is a gazebo about halfway around.

Dog owners led by their dogs, joggers, walkers, bench sitters, some looking at the lake, others reading book, mothers pushing baby carriages, homeless people with all their belongings warming themselves at picnic tables, all were on the path or nearby.

One side of the lake is bordered by a few shops including Black Dog. This area is near Munroe, a busy street. The other side of the lake has an older residential area as a border.

When I was on the far side of the lake, three Canadian geese came waddling down a residential street, honking loudly, headed for the lake. I wondered if they spent the night in someone's back garden. They certainly seemed at home.

As I walked the types of trees change, light and shadows moved in patterns. Before long I made the circuit and was back at Black Dog Café.

The coffee of the day was organic French roast. And yes, I got a pecan bar to go.

Change is the only constant in our lives. Ready or not, caused by us or not, change happens.

And sometimes that is a good thing. In my back garden, all these years, the middle pond has always been naked.

Just a preformed 12-gallon pond sitting on pavers with Buddha gracing one side. But now, change. A whole new look.

When I dismantled the small 40-gallon pond it meant removing all the big pavers that made a wall encircling the pond. And now all those stones are a wall around the middle pond.

Plus, a three-tier clay pot fountain was added along with a pelican statue and lots of plants. In addition to being attractive, all this landscaping serves as a deterrent to night marauders (raccoons) getting in the pond, destroying fish, ruining plants. So far, so good.

Speaking of night marauders, the sonic thing arrived from the Pond Guy. It works. Emits a sound I don't hear. Bella my dog does hear it, but it doesn't bother her. Must bother the raccoons. They have not been back since the sonic thing was installed.

Raccoons are currently looking elsewhere for their nightly entertainment (destructive rampages). Works for me.

Meanwhile, drum roll please, the large oval walk around the center of my garden is finally finished. It is .0693 miles long. The walk starts in sand with pavers as steps. Then choose going to the right or left on pavers set in river rock. Delightful.

Changes. New connections. Great weather. Are you outdoors yet?

Please welcome the newest member of my family – a brilliant red Mr. Betta. He resides on a kitchen counter in a one-gallon aquarium with a live plant and LED light.

Eva and Mango, my two indoor cats, have not shown any interest in the new arrival. That is a good thing.

It amazes me that this fish, bred in captivity, spending life so far in a small plastic bowl, can adapt to a new environment with old techniques.

The wild Betta splendens originated in Thailand (formerly known as Siam). This species, as well as anywhere from seventy to ninety other species of wild bettas, can be found in Cambodia, Laos, Vietnam, Brazil, Colombia, Indonesia, Malaysia, Singapore, and the Dominican Republic.

Also known as "Siamese fighting fish." If you put two males together in the same tank, things get ugly.

In the wild, bettas live in slow moving shallow waters with lots of vegetation like rice paddies and swamps. When they want to sleep (fish have sleep-wake cycles, a circadian rhythm, just like humans) they get under a leaf and relax.

The leaf acts like and upside down bed, keeps them from rising to the surface when asleep. The very first night here Mr. Betta got under a leaf and went to sleep. Amazing.

So now, he needs a nickname, a handle. Mr. Betta works for formal occasions but what about everyday swimming around? Suggestions? Let me know. The best name wins.

Speaking of names, a friend was driving several of us to lunch the day after Thanksgiving. I'm the navigator and said we'd be going down Orange then get onto Lemon. My directions were greeted with laughter.

Streets named after fruits are a long standing tropical thing here in Sarasota. The original plat from 1885 shows the city had a love affair with streets named after fruits – hence, banana, orange, mango, lemon, lime, kumquat, and strawberry.

Author/historian Jeff LaHurd said the fruit names were a lure to booster the claim by Florida Mortgage and Investment of Scotland that this area was an easy place to become a citrus farmer.

The citrus is gone. The street names remain. And then there are the flower name – magnolia, goldenrod, orchid, oleander, rose, hibiscus and – wait for it – bougainvillea.

I feel for the folks living on Bougainvillea Street, having to spell that name very carefully for any occasion that needs an address.

They may not have noticed the problem when moving in but surely over time it gets frustrating as the person on the other end of the phone, or the other side of the desk, is not going to spell Bougainvillea right the first time. Or the second time.

I DOUBLE DARE YOU to spell Bougainvillea out loud – ah, no looking at the word!

Surely anyone living on Bougainvillea would be happier on Rose or Hibiscus. Just saying.

Speaking of street names – sometimes in my travels I come across streets that bear the same name as one of my children or grandchildren. I take a photograph and send it to them. Found a street called "Martin" in Sarasota and a road named "Clara" in DeLand. Fun!

A story about St. Francis keeps tugging at the hem of my memory. When my boys were young, we lived in Seattle, Washington. Pike Place Market was a prime destination.

One day, with the youngest in a back carrier and the oldest, barely three, holding my hand, we walked along a side street near the Market.

A homeless man lay stretched out full length on the sidewalk, sleeping with his arms tucked under his head. Old newspapers covered him. Yesterday's news served as his blankets.

"Mommy, Mommy," whispered Chris, my oldest, tugging on my coat. I stopped.

Chris looked up at me, then pointed to the homeless man and asked:

"Where is St. Francis when you need him?"

Good question. We had been reading bedtime stories. One was about St. Francis and how he helped the poor.

Honestly, nobody prepares parents for these zinger questions. At least, I did not feel prepared. I always felt ten miles behind and tongue tied.

Chris was right. No St. Francis in sight. What to do? Ah ha. A lightbulb went off in my head.

"St. Francis is not here but we are," I said. "Let's go home and gather up clothes we don't wear anymore and any blankets we can."

And we did, taking them to a non-profit that gave out food and clothes to the homeless.

Perhaps it is the time of year that stirred this memory. Gift giving. Celebrations. Gatherings. But not for everyone.

Don't see St. Francis around? You can take his place. Don't see St. Nick around? You can take his place.

Last week's Wednesday Notes with fruit names for streets left out my favorite – apricot.

During apricot season in California, where I grew up, my dad always made a point of stopping at the same roadside stand along U.S. 1. They had sun dried apricots. Sweet. Wonderful. I can still smell the aroma.

And in San Rafael, California one year we lived in a house with a balcony overlooking fruit trees. We could literally stand on the balcony and pick apricots off a tree.

As for street names Verna wrote a response to last week's Wednesday Notes that beats all those fruits and flowers.

Verna once lived in a Colorado neighborhood where the streets were all named after characters from King Arthur tales.

They lived on Sir Galahad. It intersected with Excalibur. Now that is an elegant address!

Wednesday Notes, December 15, 2021

There is a new museum in St. Petersburg, Florida and it will knock your socks off – at least it did mine.

The Museum of the American Arts and Crafts Movement on Fourth Street North joins a busy downtown waterfront arts district.

Grand, soaring, full of light and intriguing layout, this building gets your attention both outside and inside. Five stories tall, the museum avoids the usual angst of parking problems by providing a garage right next door – at a very reasonable rate of $1 an hour.

The clear message: stay a while. And stay we did.

In America from 1890 to 1930 the Arts and Crafts movement was strongly counterculture – seeking an alternative to mass produced goods by designing and creating objects both functional and beautiful.

A Tiffany lamp, for example, stands on its own. It hardly matters that the light bulbs (dim as they were then) are turned on or not.

Nature motifs prevail. Beautiful craftmanship triumphs. Whoever curated this museum knows the value of letting pieces stand and speak on their own. Like this chair.

A splendid spiral staircase winds up five floors. You will get all your daily steps in. Or take the elevator.

Every floor is different. Decorative tile in one space, fireplaces in another. One wall showcases pottery fired in many different kilns – all in breathtaking shades of green.

Another area has tiles of different kinds, all with identification who did them, what kiln, what purpose they served.

The second floor sets the arts and crafts tone right away with an installation saved from demolition – the 1912 entry hall from the James A. Culbertson House in Pasadena California designed by architects Charles and Henry Greene.

We realized at once that this first visit would barely scratch the surface. We were drawn from one "oh my" thing to another, walking around in a daze.

This is a museum to come back to again and again building in lots of time to read labels, absorb beauty and revel in the grand designs.

For deep immersion, there is a MAACM audio tour available on the IOS app store or Google play.

Planning suggestions: We bought tickets ahead online, just show the barcode for admission. Museum is closed on

Mondays. Rest of the week hours are 10 a.m. to 4 p.m. Check website for current times and days before you visit.

Getting our fill of visuals and history after five floors, we needed a lunch break badly.

Across the street is the Tap Room at the Hollander Hotel with lots of covered outside seating. Lovely lunch. Normally dessert is not on my menu but when the waitress said all their desserts come from a bakery in Tarpon Springs, well, that did it.

My mantra – if the Greeks are cooking, just show up. Dessert arrived. We had key lime tarts and they were memorable.

Meanwhile, back home, readers of Wednesday Notes really responded to naming Mr. Betta.

The winning name is Betta O'Rourke, submitted by both Kate G. and Yvonne J.

You all had way too much fun coming up with fish names. Here are some: Betta O'Rourke, Alpha Betta (Al for short), Than Ever, Swimmy, Traveler, Walker, Flash, Hephaestus (fire god), Don'TchaTomato, Bewtta Bettafly, TobiasBetta (ToBe), Better Betta (BB), Flame, Red, Flipper, Sam, Stoic, Fanboy, Otto Know Betta, Naraja, Fish, Flaming Lips, Moe Betta.

My betta enjoyed hearing all the names from readers, but he was much more interested in the food jar that I had in my hand. Quite enjoyable watching him swim around and show off his lovely fins and tail.

Ready or not, Christmas comes. May our hearts grow three times bigger, filled with love, hope, joy, and peace.

Mango the cat heard a rumor Santa stuffed the pet stocking with catnip toys. Sure enough, catnip appeared.

I had quite forgotten how much that boy likes catnip.

Ah, if only making someone happy was as easy as the gift of a catnip toy.

Looking ahead to 2022 – hope for health, a calming of the chaos around the world and may there be many chances to connect with each other in meaningful ways.

See you the first Wednesday of 2022.

# Acknowledgements

Kudos and namaste to my editor Sue Crawford who manages to keep me on the right style path. At the beginning of the Wednesday Notes, Dawn Finnerty liked the blog. She saved each week's missive in a folder. One year later, changing out computers, I lost all Notes for 2020. And Dawn came to the rescue. She had them all in that folder. Salvation. A huge round of applause to all Wednesday Notes readers. You have encouraged me, engaged with Wednesday Notes, and fortified by love and laughter; we walk this journey side by side. I am grateful for every one of you.

# Books by Lucy Tobias

50 Great Walks in Florida

Florida Gardens Gone Wild

Florida Gardens Gone Wild(er)

The Zen of Florida Gardening

Circle the Center Labyrinths in Florida

# Books for children

Mary Margaret Manatee

The adventures of a young Florida Manatee

(English and Spanish)

# Stories in Anthologies

Beach Reads

Chicken Soup for the Soul:

My Very Good Very Bad Dog

# Poems in Anthologies

Landfall

Amelia . . .A shimmer on the water

A whisper on the wind

Thank you
for reading this book

Please support independent
bookstores and all libraries

Visit www.LucyTobias.com to view Lucy's books and
subscribe to Wednesday Notes. Email: greatwalks@gmail.com

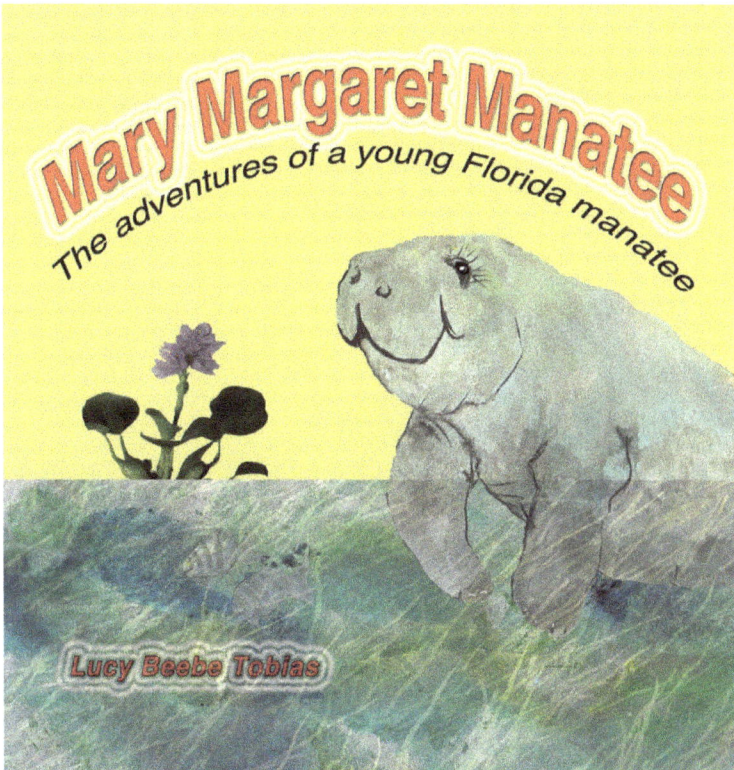

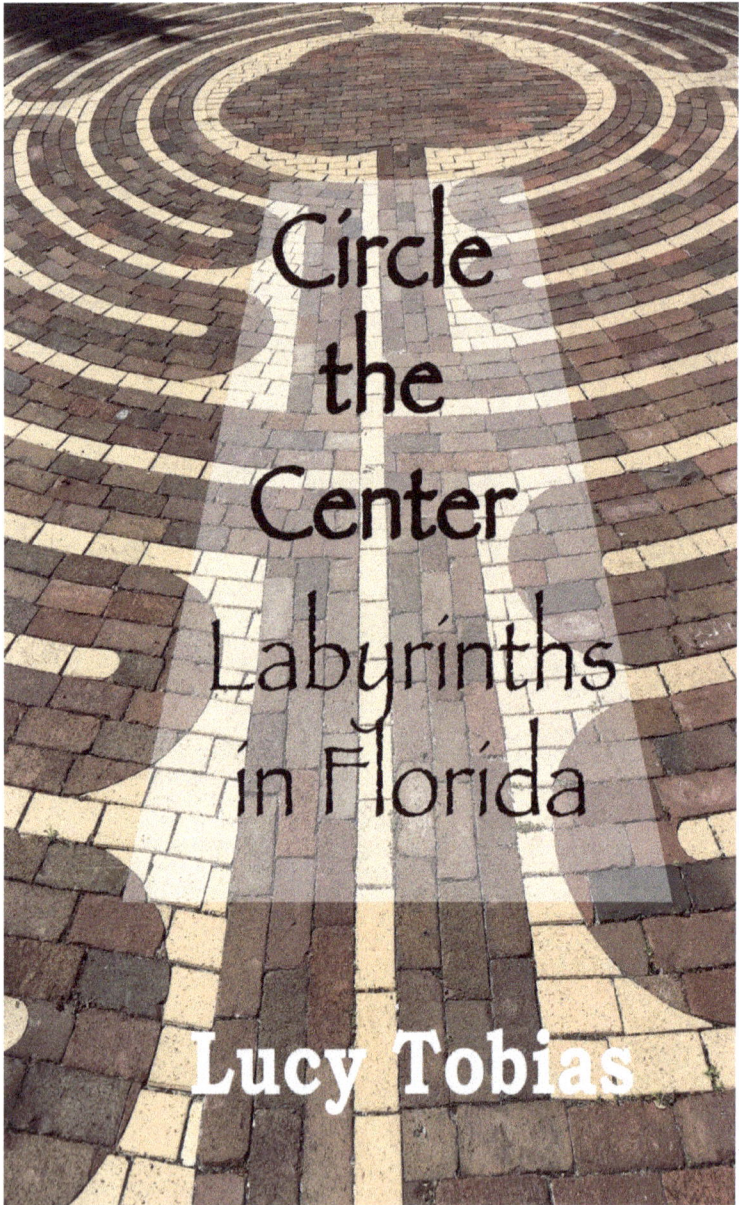

Circle
the
Center

Labyrinths
in Florida

Lucy Tobias

WILD FLORIDA

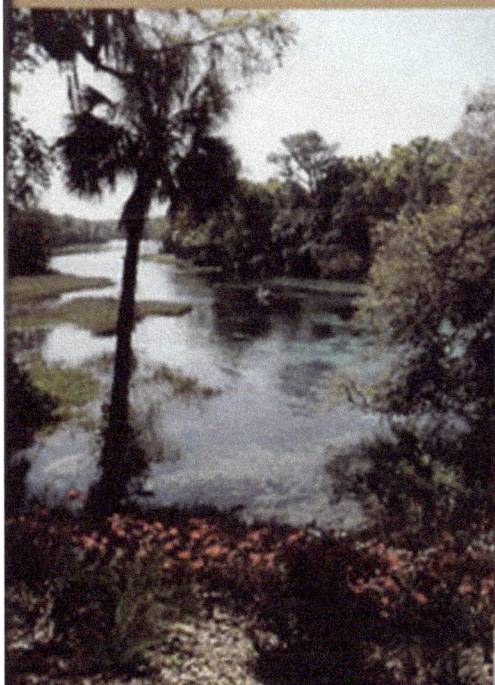

50
Great
Walks
in
Florida

Lucy Beebe Tobias

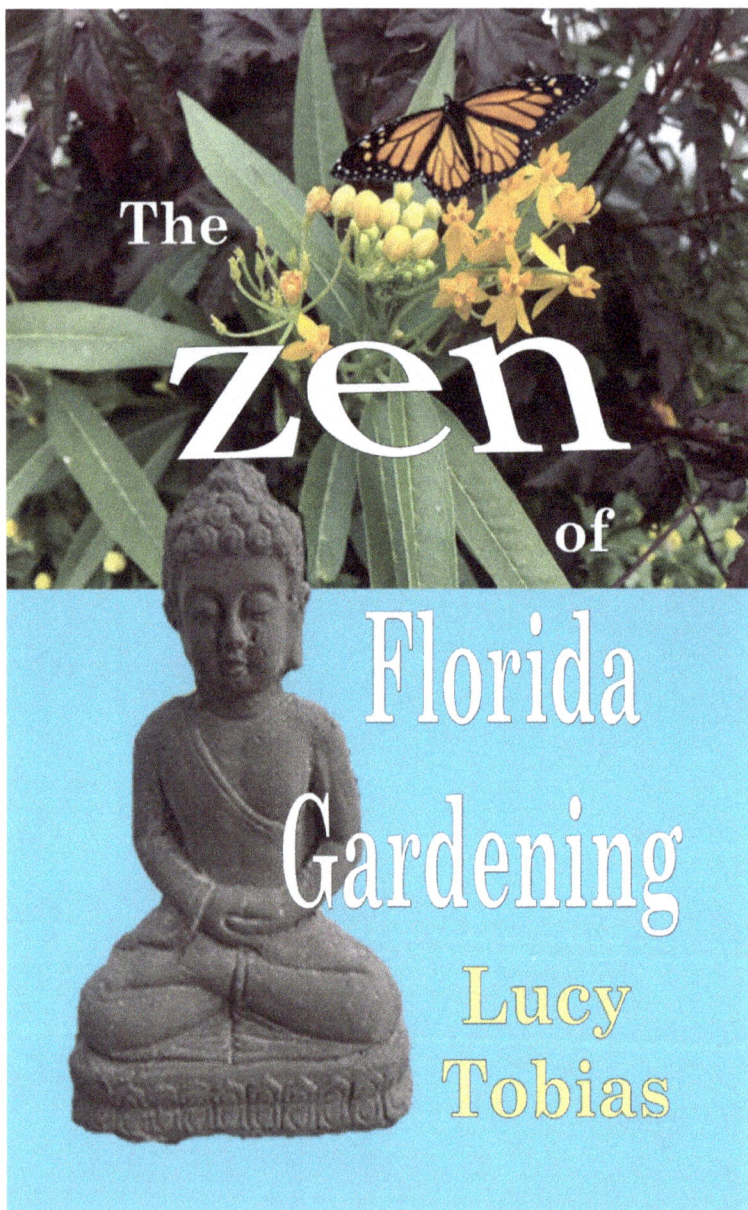

# The

# zen

## of

# Florida

# Gardening

## Lucy
## Tobias